Creativity, Activity, Service (CAS)

for the IB Diploma

An essential guide for students

John Cannings, Maria Ines Piaggio, Peter Muir and Tom Brodie

CAMBRIDGE
UNIVERSITY PRESS

CAMBRIDGE
UNIVERSITY PRESS

University Printing House, Cambridge CB2 8BS, United Kingdom

Cambridge University Press is part of the University of Cambridge.

It furthers the University's mission by disseminating knowledge in the pursuit of education, learning and research at the highest international levels of excellence.

Information on this title: www.cambridge.org

This work has been developed independently from and is not endorsed by the International Baccalaureate (IB).

© Cambridge University Press 2015

This publication is in copyright. Subject to statutory exception and to the provisions of relevant collective licensing agreements, no reproduction of any part may take place without the written permission of Cambridge University Press.

First published 2015

Printed in Poland by Opolgraf

A catalogue record for this publication is available from the British Library

ISBN 978-1-107-56034-5 Paperback

Cambridge University Press has no responsibility for the persistence or accuracy of URLs for external or third-party internet websites referred to in this publication, and does not guarantee that any content on such websites is, or will remain, accurate or appropriate. Information regarding prices, travel timetables, and other factual information given in this work is correct at the time of first printing but Cambridge University Press does not guarantee the accuracy of such information thereafter.

Acknowledgements
The authors and publishers acknowledge the following sources of copyright material and are grateful for the permissions granted. While every effort has been made, it has not always been possible to identify the sources of all the material used, or to trace all copyright holders. If any omissions are brought to our notice, we will be happy to include the appropriate acknowledgements on reprinting.

pp. 7, 8, 9, 16, 27, 58, 65, 66, 70, 112, 113, 125, 126, 130, 134, 156, 163, 164, 175, 176, 177, 209, 210, 218, 226, 227, 228, 229, 230, 240, 241, 243, 244 © The International Baccalaureate Organization; p. 33 www.un.org/ millenniumgoals, © UNDP Brazil; p. 63 'The Reflective Cycle' from Gibbs G (1988) *Learning by doing: a guide to teaching and learning methods.* published by Oxford: Further Education Unit, Oxford Polytechnic. reproduced by permission of Oxford Centre for Staff and Learning Development (OCSLD); p. 75 © 2008 National Youth Leadership Council, St. Paul, MN. www.nylc.org. All rights reserved; p.84–85 interview and ConCert logo http:// www.concertcambodia.org/volunteer.html; p. 179 © ManageBac (www.managebac.com); p. 179 gibbonedu. org © 2011 Ross Parker (rossparker.org), software developed at International College Hong Kong; p. 193 http:// helpingthemotherteresasociety.weebly.com/ © Jehona Gutaj, Ella Liskens, Sarah McCowan; p. 214-5 http://www. casel.org/social-and-emotional-learning/core-competencies, © The Collaborative for Academic, Social, and Emotional Learning; p. 221 © stus.com. All rights reserved.

Cover photograph: Belinda Images/Superstock

Photographs
p. 8 © María Inés Piaggio; p. 9 © Tom Brodie; p. 10 © María Inés Piaggio; p. 12 © Shutterstock.com/Rudie Strummer; p. 21 © Shutterstock.com/Goodluz; p. 35 © Shutterstock.com/Rawpixel; p. 42 © Shutterstock. com/Matej Kastelic; p. 44 © DeeLee Photo Design; p. 59 © Shutterstock.com/auremar; p. 63 © Shutterstock. com/Asfia; p. 72 © Pedro Schmitt Del Solar (Colegio Alpamayo); p. 73 © Shutterstock.com/Ryan Rodrick Beiler; p. 93 © Shutterstock.com/Alexander Raths; p. 107 Stock photo © Steve Debenport; p. 114 © Stephane Bidouze /Shutterstock.com; p. 128 © Jeffrey McLean; p. 136 © Jorge Bendezú; p. 143 © Jeffrey McLean; p. 148 © Peter Muir; p. 151 © DeeLee Photo Design; p. 155 © Shutterstock.com/somsak suwanput; p. 157 © Katrina Woodford (United World College, Singapore); p. 186 © Tonbridge Grammar School; p. 188 © Cheltenham, Ladies' College; p. 189 © iStockphoto/DNY59; p. 192 © International School of Kuala Lumpa, Malaysia; p. 206 © Shutterstock.com/Monkey Business Images; p. 217 © International School of Kuala Lumpur; p. 227 © Shutterstock.com/Anatoli Styf; p. 237 © Shutterstock.com/wavebreakmedia.

Contents

Introduction to
the book

Creativity, Activity and Service (CAS) is meant to give you, the student, a chance to have a set of worthwhile and fun experiences that can be the highlight of your IB Diploma. Many graduates of the IB Diploma programme have shared with us that they feel some of their greatest achievements and learning came from CAS. They remember the special moments they had, trying to teach people English or working in an old people's home, and how much the residents looked forward to them coming each week. They say they got to know themselves and their fellow students much better when they worked together on a service project together. These anecdotes highlight their willingness to go outside of their comfort zone, try something and not give up. CAS is not an abstract activity: you are meant to 'get your hands dirty' and actually do things!

The Diploma Graduates who spoke to me all agreed that carrying out service activities changed them as people for the better. They said that working with other people helped them to be more aware of other people's feelings and also to learn about themselves. That is one of the challenges that you face over the next 18 months. In this book we shall outline many different examples of service.

A high point of the programme for many CAS students is the project that they will carry out. The CAS stages framework will help you to plan and carry out projects much better than in the past. We offer you some practical suggestions about projects and some activities to help you plan your own project.

This book supplements the 2015 CAS Guide and reflects the changes therein. It should help you to understand the requirements of CAS and has been written with you, the student, in mind. CAS still focuses on experiential learning, which requires you to reflect on the experiences that you have while doing it. There are many examples taken from students' personal reflections in the book and some photographs of them in action.

You will be encouraged in the book to see that CAS is not an isolated part of the IB Diploma, but that the skills and values developed in it will help your academic subjects. CAS encourages you to see the links between what you learn in class and the experiences you have outside of it.

There are many activities in the book that are designed to help clarify your thoughts about CAS and to challenge your own assumptions and ideas. This book is one that you will probably 'dip into' as you need ideas throughout the IB Diploma course. The authors have all had experience as CAS Coordinators and have provided examples from the three CAS regions (Europe and the Middle East, the Americas and Asia/Pacific).

We wish you a great CAS experience!

The nature of CAS

Alec Peterson, the first director of the IB, summarised the aims of the IB succinctly when he said:

The Educational aims of the IB programme: to develop to their fullest potential the powers of each individual to understand, to modify and to enjoy his or her environment, both inner and outer, in its physical, social, moral, aesthetic and spiritual aspects. *(Alec Peterson, 2003)*

From the very start, the IB Diploma Programme has been concerned with developing you as a whole person.

The key features of CAS from the IB's viewpoint are:

- a focus not just on what you have done, but how you have developed as an individual as a result of your involvement in CAS
- a move away from service being something you do for others, to doing something with others for mutual benefits
- a conscientious approach from you as a CAS participant to learn more about the communities with whom you work. More than this, to also contribute to the various communities in which you live.

For these reasons and more, CAS is considered one of the central pillars of the IB Diploma Programme. In many ways it is the IB Mission Statement in action, a factor that clearly distinguishes it from other university entrance courses. CAS really is the experiential part of the IB Diploma Programme that supports its claim to educate the whole person.

As American psychologist David Kolb said, 'Learning is the process whereby knowledge is created through the transformation of experience.' John Dewey was the first person to write about experiential education, and he simply said 'Experience plus reflection equals learning.'

1

1.01 The purpose of this book

1 To help students understand the new CAS guidelines by explaining the language and ideas behind the guide in a student-friendly way (Chapter 1).

2 To present CAS as a blueprint for personal development in the IB Diploma Programme (Chapter 1).

3 To provide you, the student, with criteria and models to help you decide what is a valid CAS experience – in the authors' experience, this has always been something that has challenged students and IB teachers (Chapter 1).

4 To introduce you to the CAS stages model that will help you to plan and carry out CAS experiences and projects (Chapters 2 and 6).

5 To provide you with ideas about how to reflect on your CAS experiences and make this a more rewarding and richer experience (Chapter 3).

6 To demonstrate the links between CAS and the other parts of the core and provide you with a strategy for preparing a TOK presentation based on a valid and authentic CAS experience (Chapter 5).

7 To provide you with some thoughts of experienced CAS Coordinators about the programme (you will find this throughout the book).

8 To provide case studies and snapshots of good CAS practice from each of the three regions of the IB (IB in Africa, Europe and the Middle East, IB of the Americas and IB Asia/Pacific) (you will find this throughout the book).

9 To provide you with some ideas on how to develop your CAS portfolio and demonstrate your achievements in CAS (Chapter 7).

10 To show you the approaches to learning skills and how you might develop these through CAS (Chapter 9).

11 To show you how CAS relates to learner profile and how you can further develop these qualities.

Key point: This is a book that you can consult as you work through the Diploma Programme, and it will help to make your CAS a more meaningful and fun experience.

1.02 What do the C, A and S stand for?

C – Creativity: 'exploring and extending ideas leading to an original or interpretive product or performance'.

CAS Guide (2015), page 8, IBO

This is a great opportunity to do something that you have always wanted to do, or take things to a new level of accomplishment. It could be to finally put a band together.

CAS SNAPSHOT

Creativity could also be getting up on stage. At Discovery College in Hong Kong, a group of students wrote a play, set in Germany during the Second World War, which became the school production for that year. The students developed the script, designed the set and costumes, and collaborated with their peers to develop the score and visual effects.

Creativity could also mean to learn how to salsa or tango, create your own app or website, write poetry, or develop a plan to reduce your family's greenhouse gas emissions. It could be to take something you are already doing to a new level, or to try something you have never done before. The list of possibilities is endless – what is important is that you are engaged in the creative thought process.

1

Figure 1.1 Students working creatively, painting a mural at an InterCAS (a conference for CAS students held annually in South America).

A – Activity: 'physical exertion contributing to a healthy lifestyle'.
CAS Guide (2015), page 8, IBO

The inclusion of this strand of CAS is to encourage you to do something physical that will benefit your wellbeing, to participate in something that you will enjoy and, hopefully, continue for the rest of your life. You might take up yoga or Pilates, go to the gym, or learn to dance salsa, or you might choose an outdoor activity like climbing, continue with a sport you already like or try a new sport.

CAS SNAPSHOT

Students at Skagerak International School in Norway had the opportunity to learn the basics of climbing, and after this they ventured into ice climbing. This is an activity that they want to continue after they leave school.

Figure 1.2 A student ice climbing in Norway.

S – Service: 'collaborative and reciprocal engagement with the community in response to an authentic need'.

CAS Guide (2015), page 8, IBO

In CAS, service is meant to be a social act, working with people outside of the family and not for profit. The aim is for you to contribute in your own way to making the world a better place and it will require some research to identify a specific need in the community. The next step requires collaboration with the community to see what you can do to service this particular need.

It is important to stress the idea of reciprocity and exchange (to avoid paternalism) and this, in our opinion, is the most challenging and yet rewarding of the CAS areas. It demands from you important social skills and a positive attitude. It requires you to develop a relationship with people in order to carry out a task. People with whom you are working will soon pick up from your body language and enthusiasm how keen you are to be involved.

Because Service has a direct impact on others, it is very important for it to be well-planned to ensure that this impact is positive. Chapter 6 on working with others, outlines what some negative impacts may be, and includes some guidance on how to avoid them.

CAS SNAPSHOT

Margrit and Anna realised the need for people to go and read for blind people, so they signed up with the Red Cross to do this on a weekly basis. First they had to do a preparatory training course, which included being blindfolded for half a day in the home to get an understanding of what it is like to be blind.

Figure 1.3 IB Diploma Programme Mexican students working with Habitat for Humanity in Mexico.

1.03 Changes to CAS

The *CAS Guide* published in 2015 has made a number of important changes to this central part of the Diploma Programme:

1 There is no reference to an hour requirement, rather a continuous commitment to CAS over a duration of 18 months.

2 The three strands of CAS are now named Creativity, Activity and Service.

3 We now refer to CAS events as CAS experiences.

4 CAS experience guidelines have been introduced to help clarify what is, and what is not CAS.

5 You have to show evidence of having met seven learning outcomes at least once during the IB Diploma Programme. The evidence for this should be included in a CAS portfolio.

6 You are expected to use the CAS stages model in planning and carrying out CAS experiences (the five stages are: investigation, preparation, action, reflection and demonstration).

7 You are expected to collaborate with other students, to plan, initiate and carry out a CAS project in one or more of the CAS strands. This project should have a duration of at least one month.

8 There is a heavy emphasis on your reflection. However, this reflection can be in a variety of different media, NOT just in a written form.

9 CAS should involve enjoyment, choice and engagement. The CAS experiences chosen by you should be fun and beneficial.

10 You are expected to keep a portfolio of your CAS engagement. It can be in electronic form and is expected to include reflections in various formats, and other evidence of CAS experiences. Vital to the CAS portfolio is evidence of achievement in the learning outcomes.

1

1.04 Why are there no points for CAS in the IB Diploma Programme?

One of the main purposes of having CAS in the IB Diploma Programme is to encourage personal growth and development. It is impossible to objectively quantify this, and it has been argued that it is not something that we should attempt to do. Each student has a unique starting and finishing point in CAS, and trying to make a judgement about the distance they have come, and the benefits they have received from it, is difficult to judge even after students have left school.

1.05 What CAS can do for you

The value of CAS:
- your chance for personal development
- an opportunity to learn new skills
- a chance for taking action and making a difference to improve life conditions in different communities
- a chance to develop your language skills
- a chance to meet and interact with different cultures
- a chance to work in a team to problem solve.

Figure 1.4   CAS can help you to develop into a special individual.

Creativity, Activity and Service has been described as being the heart of the IB Diploma Programme. It provides Diploma students with an opportunity to develop skills and talents, as well as areas for growth, and also to work to make the world a better place through active involvement in the community. You will be expected to have a range of different experiences, be able to keep a record of them and indicate what you learnt from them. Above all, CAS presents a chance for you to develop as a whole person, according to the IB learner profile.

This is a rare opportunity to challenge yourself and develop. It is an aspect of the IB Diploma Programme that sets it apart from many systems and makes it attractive to universities and employers. Your 18-month CAS programme gives you the opportunity of doing things that you have always wanted to do, but never had the opportunity to do so.

It is important to remember the words of William George Plunkett:

Three things that never come back: the harsh word, the spent arrow, the lost opportunity.

The IB Diploma Programme is a unique time in your life that will make a difference to you and those around you, so don't miss out on this special opportunity!

The challenge of developing as a whole person

When you have a wide range of challenging pursuits for CAS – things that take you out of your comfort zone – it will help you to clarify and develop your own set of values, contributing to your ethical identity.

a   Work out what is really important to you in life and how to use your talents to make a better world. To do this you must be able to reflect on the things that you do (this means much more than writing endlessly about your every move) and consider 'is this what I really think is right for me?'

1

This quote from the Chinese philosopher Confucius highlights the value of reflection:

By three methods can we learn wisdom: First by reflection, which is the noblest, second by imitation, which is the easiest, and third by experience, which is the bitterest.

What Confucius was emphasising was how important it is to learn by reflecting on our experiences. He was also making the point that when we act without thinking or reflecting, we make mistakes and this is the hardest way of actually learning something. This approach by Confucius is in line with the approach of CAS, where we want to plan our future actions on the basis of what we have learnt from our past actions.

b   Develop a sense of international mindedness.

c   Grasp the opportunity to practise and use your second language (Language B in the Diploma Programme). This may come from working with migrants in your local community or tutoring local children.

d   Understand and develop awareness of other cultures. No matter where we live on our planet, we have the chance to work with people from different parts of the world and appreciate their culture. In Dubai we have schools that help the migrant workers on the building sites. In Singapore students can work with domestic helpers from abroad. In North America students can involve themselves with indigenous communities. In Latin America students join and work with native communities in a mutually enriching exchange.

e   Deal with issues of global importance in your local community. For example, in many Latin American countries, CAS students engage in adult literacy programmes.

1.06 Now, how about you?

- What do you want to do after you graduate from school?
- What inter-personal skills (how well do you get on with people from different backgrounds) do you think you need to develop to achieve this?
- What special creative interests do you want to develop (as a musician, actor, set designer, visual artist, video producer, photographer...)?
- Are you already doing something in this area that you want to develop?
- What sports or individual fitness activities do you want to develop further?
- Are there any new things you want to try out (ice-climbing, canoeing, skiing, surfing, wave-ski, rock climbing, salsa, zumba)?
- Is there a group where you are already helping out as a volunteer (Red Cross, Red Crescent, Greenpeace, Caritas, an old people's home, abandoned children, orphans, disabled people)?
- Which group would you like to work with to help serve others?
- How are you going to use your second language as part of CAS?

1

1.07 Some strategies for deciding what is a valid CAS experience

What is a CAS experience?

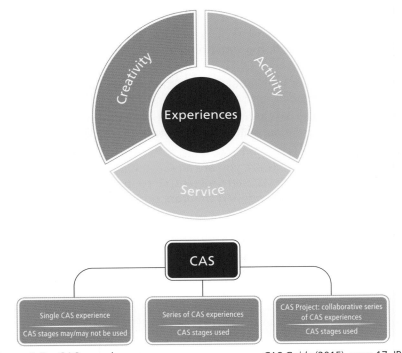

Figure 1.5 CAS experiences

CAS Guide (2015), page 17, IBO

CAS experiences should:
1 involve one or more of the CAS Strands – C, A or S
2 be a chance for personal growth through a new challenge
3 give you a chance to demonstrate some of the qualities and attributes of the learner profile
4 give you a chance to have fun
5 not be part of your Diploma Programme.

CAS Guide (2015), pages 14–15, IBO

Three CAS student proposals which meet CAS requirements

CAS Proposal 1:

Creating an educational app: Creativity

Proposal for a CAS experience: To create an educational app for iOS which will be unique and new.

Is it going to lead to personal development? Yes, I will have to learn how to code to make such an app, and I am going to have to make some graphics with it; neither of which have I done before. I think this will mean I will have to contact people on the internet that I have never met before and get their support/help.

Which strand of C, A and S will it fit? Definitely Creativity as this will result in the production of a new product that will be a result of my creative thinking and a unique piece of work. My explanations of how the app might work will also be a service to people that want to use my app.

Learner profile attributes that I shall be developing as a result of my participation

Inquirer: I have to find out how to encode my app and develop it.

Communicator: I am going to have to communicate with people to help develop the app and also to promote it when it is completed. In doing this I am also going to satisfy a **CAS learning outcome of collaborating with others**.

Courageous: I am going to take on something which is brand new to me and I may risk failure.

Knowledgeable: I am going to become knowledgeable about apps.

Principled: I must make sure that I do not steal someone else's idea.

Thinkers: This will force me to think creatively and originally and solve several problems.

Part of my Course: No, this will definitely not be part of my IB Diploma Programme.

Will it be fun to do this? Yes, I definitely think this will be enjoyable and a real challenge for me.

CAS Proposal 2:

Dancing hip-hop: Activity

Proposal for a CAS experience: I want to learn to dance hip-hop. I am going to go to a course at Billi's dance school. For me it will be like a fitness activity as I shall be going three times a week for two hours at a time. Maybe, I shall become good enough to join in the school's 'I've got talent show' in May next year.

Which strand of C, A and S will it fit? Hip-hop dancing is pretty demanding and I think that it would fit the requirements for Activity as I shall be doing this on a regular basis. In addition, I shall be creating my own dances so it will also be creative.

Is the experience going to lead to personal development? No doubt, as I have never had the chance to learn how to do this. At the moment I am not having much regular exercise and I think that this would be really fun. It will give me that chance to learn some new and exciting.

Learner profile attributes that I shall be developing as a result of our work/my participation

Knowledgeable: I am going to learn some new techniques of hip-hop dancing.

Communicator: With my teachers and other students who will help me to practise new steps and techniques.

Courageous: I want to develop my own style that I can use with my friends when I go clubbing.

Balanced: This will help me to achieve a better balance in my life as I shall be doing some physical activity and something I enjoy.

Is hip-hop dancing part of my course for the IB Diploma Programme? Sadly, it is not even part of the physical education programme that we have to do. There is no chance to do any form of dance in our programme, which focuses on sports and outdoor activities like rock climbing (I am scared of heights) or kayaking.

Is it going to be enjoyable? No doubt about that. My best friend goes to this dance school and she says the leaders are really good and just love trying new things out. That's what I want to do – push the limits a bit and be outstanding on the dance floor. If this is what I can do through CAS it's not going to be so bad after all.

CAS Proposal 3:

A Service activity

Proposal for a CAS experience: I want to go and work with Lighthouse, a charity that helps to provide food for homeless people in our city. That means on Friday nights I shall go and meet the team at their office and help make some sandwiches and coffee that we are going to distribute. The team then goes around the city in a van and helps to distribute food. Each day when I come to school I see these homeless people appear from their cardboard boxes where they sleep. Lighthouse require us to make a six-month commitment to it. My parents are happy for me to be involved as they have read about the charity.

What strand of C, A and S will this fit? This is going to be a Service where I can help those in my community who are not so fortunate. I want to do something to try to make life a bit better for these people. One day there was a girl I saw who had been sleeping out that I recognised from my primary school class; this really touched me.

Will there be personal development? It's the first time that I have really wanted to commit to something that was not just for my own interest. I think it will be good for me to work with people from a different background to my own as I have been privileged in so many ways.

Learner profile qualities

Caring: I think this will help me to be more aware of the needs and feelings of others, and I hope to make a positive contribution to others less fortunate than myself.

Reflective: The experience of doing this will help me to understand my strengths and limitations.

Open-minded: This will help me to understand the culture and values of others better.

Courageous: This will help me to approach this new challenge with some new fortitude.

1.08 Strategies for turning an experience into a CAS experience

CAS Proposal 1:

Proposal for a CAS experience: I want to include walking as part of Activity. I do this three times a week.

Suggestions to make this more appropriate for CAS: Most CAS Coordinators would probably reject this proposal as it stands, as not being a really challenging activity. Now let us see how it could be developed so that it becomes a valid CAS experience. How can it fit the requirements for a CAS activity?

Set yourself some goals for your walking exercise. Some examples could be:

1   I have measured my walk and I currently cover a distance of 2 km in an hour. My goal is that in two months' time I shall be able to walk 3 km in an hour. In six months' time I want to be able to walk 4 km in an hour.

2   I am going to get a step measurer and see how many steps I take in an hours walk. In two months' time I am going to try to increase the number of steps I take by 25%.

3   To make the walking become fairly rigorous, I am going to get myself some Nordic walking sticks and join a group of people in my neighbourhood that walk each day.

Evidence of this actually taking place:

1   I shall agree to having a timed distance walk at the end of two months to show my improvement.

2   I shall take some dated photos with my mobile phone showing me in action.

3   I might be able to take part in a long distance hike, e.g. the length of Ho Chi Minh trail in Vietnam, part of the Cornwall coastal path in the UK or the Appalachian walking trail from Maine to Eastern Canada.

CAS Proposal 2:

Proposal for a CAS experience: I want to go and work in a hotel as a waiter/waitress, receptionist, cook. I would like this to be a Service.

Suggestions to make this more appropriate for CAS: In submitting a proposal such as this, the student would often add that they would not be paid for their work, and as such this is to be considered as volunteering. Motivation for this is often so that the student can gain the experience in the hospitality industry that they need to secure a position in a hotel school after graduation.

Most CAS Coordinators would not accept this as being a service. Rather than being an unpaid social service as the CAS Guide suggests, this is more of an internship in a particular role that provides free labour for a company. How can this be turned into a CAS experience?

1 Create a handbook or blog about the experience of working in the hotel or restaurant, and highlight the strengths and weaknesses of the career. Make this available to students in the school who would be contemplating a career in the catering business. It could outline:
   a working conditions
   b different roles within the business
   c how the business is organised
   d what qualities employers are looking for from employees.

2 If you are working in the kitchen, create a cookbook with pictures of the food that is produced. The book should have very clear instructions about the ingredients, equipment and steps needed to follow this. You might also demonstrate what you have learnt by creating the dish.

Figure 1.6 Working in a professional kitchen.

CAS Proposal 3:

Proposal for a CAS experience: I intend joining a beach clean up on a Saturday morning.

Suggestions to make this more appropriate for CAS: Though well intended, this idea is not challenging enough for the average Diploma Programme student. As indicated by the guidelines for a CAS experience, CAS must provide opportunities to develop the attributes of the IB learner profile. The experience should also allow for development of personal interests, skills and/or talents, and provide new possibilities or challenges. It could also be said that although one-off activities can certainly be a part of a student's CAS portfolio, planned experiences of a longer duration are recommended for a more engaging CAS programme. How can this be turned into a CAS experience?

1 You could be involved in a number of beach clean-ups over a number of weekends.

2 You could encourage others to join you in cleaning up the beach. Perhaps you could even organise your own beach clean-up events.

3 Conduct some research on the impact of pollution on the marine environment, and share your findings with the local community. You could perhaps have a stand in the school foyer, informing the school community about the issue.

CAS Proposal 4:

Proposal for a CAS experience: I ride my bicycle to school and would like this to be an Activity.

Suggestions to make this more appropriate for CAS: While it is true this is a physically active pursuit, simply exerting energy does not necessarily mean the involvement should be considered as Activity. A point to consider is that if this student has been riding their bicycle to school for a number of years, would the experience be challenging, or provide a chance for them to develop the attributes of the IB learner profile? How can this be turned into a CAS experience?

1 Set yourself a challenging goal to improve your fitness, and develop a plan to reach this goal. This could perhaps be to cycle a certain distance under a given time.

2 Consider entering a cycling race or event, and train to prepare yourself for it.

CAS Proposal 5:

Proposal for a CAS experience: Attending an arts exhibition.

Suggestions to make this more appropriate for CAS: Though attending an arts exhibition may inspire creative thought or action, passive involvement such as this does not constitute CAS. The guidelines for a CAS experience outlined in the *CAS Guide* indicate that this proposal is not acceptable as CAS as you are expected to produce a product. How can this be turned into a CAS experience?

1 You could create a piece of art, or a number of pieces, and hold your own exhibition.

2 You could create a guide for those who visit the exhibition, with your own points of view on the different pieces you observed.

1.09 Some questions to ask yourself to help minimise risks from carrying out CAS

Self-assessing the risks

Some CAS experiences may expose you to certain risks. While it is important that your CAS Coordinator considers these risks, you too can be involved in taking steps to reduce your chances of being harmed. The following section outlines some questions that will help you assess some risks. As CAS students operate in many different contexts and laws throughout the world, it is impossible to mention every possible eventuality you would have to consider. Many schools will have a much more formalised form of risk assessment that you will have to complete before your CAS Coordinator sanctions your CAS experience or project.

Climatic

1 What clothing will I have to wear if it is:
   - hot
   - cold
   - wet?

2 Will I need to wear any form of sunblock, sunglasses?

Environmental

1 Is there any need to protect against insects, reptiles or predators?

2 Do I need to have vaccinations/medications to work in this environment?

3 Is there safe access to the worksite?

4 Do I need to wear protective clothing and or boots?

5 Is the workplace safe from avalanches/rock/mudslides or other hazards?

Social

1 Are your parents aware of what you are going to do, and do they agree with it?

2 Will you have adult supervision when you are carrying out the activity?

3 Can you travel safely to and from the experience?

4 If the experience is to occur in non-contact time at school, has the school agreed to you carrying out the experience at that time?

Section 2.01 in Chapter 2 will cover risk assessment in more detail.

1.10 Review of Chapter 1

1   What do you think the main benefit of CAS is for you?

2   What do you have to do to meet the CAS requirements for the IB Diploma Programme?

3   Can you define the three strands of CAS in your own words?

4   What is a CAS experience?

5   How can you tell if your proposal is valid for CAS?

6   What do the examples of successful CAS proposals have in common?

7   Why do you need to consider the risks of an experience before undertaking it?

1.11 A summary of this chapter

- Information about what CAS is and some definitions.

- Some thoughts about what CAS can do for you.

- Some strategies for defining a valid CAS experience.

- A strategy for turning an experience into a CAS experience.

- Some case studies of CAS from different parts of the world.

- Some questions to ask yourself to help minimise harm from carrying out CAS.

The CAS stages framework

The CAS stages is a suggested method for approaching your CAS programme, designed to support planning for and implementing CAS involvement. Much more than simply an extension of the experiential learning model, it is a process that will assist you in getting the most out of your CAS experiences and projects. It is recommended that the CAS stages be followed for all CAS experiences.

Experiential learning: learning from experience; enhancing the understanding gained from an experience through reflection.

This chapter will explain each of the five CAS stages:

- Investigation
- Preparation
- Action
- Reflection
- Demonstration.

It will provide you with some examples of the framework in action and include some practical activities to support your understanding of the use of the five stages.

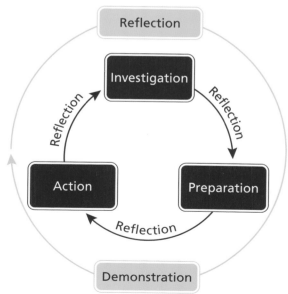

Figure 2.1   A model on the CAS stages.   *CAS Guide* (2015), page 16, IBO

2

The CAS stages are designed to assist you in seeking opportunities for CAS, to help with developing plans for CAS experiences, to help you celebrate and share what you have done, and to help you with your reflections. Ideally the CAS stages are to be utilised in the early stages of a CAS experience. In many cases the Investigation stage may guide you in finding a new experience to pursue.

Though the design of the CAS stages allows for them to be followed sequentially, this may not always be the case. In some situations when you are already participating in a CAS experience (such as the Action stage) you may need to go back to the Preparation stage to help refine or improve your planning. You may also find yourself in a situation where you would benefit from investigating more about the CAS experience in which you are preparing to engage. Additionally, reflection may be done throughout the process (as outlined in Chapter 3) you should not wait until you have finished your involvement in a CAS experience before you reflect. Ongoing reflection can help refine plans, develop questions for further investigation and guide future involvement.

As we move on to look at each of the CAS stages in more detail, consider how you might already have used the five stages of CAS, though not necessarily by those named.

The CAS stages: a framework to assist students in planning and carrying out their CAS experiences / projects. The five stages are Investigation, Preparation, Action, Reflection and Demonstration.

2.01 Investigation

In most cases, this is the recommended way of commencing your CAS engagement – by finding out details of what you might want to do, and, with regard to service, which needs exist in the community that you could address. Your investigation involves clarifying ideas, building factual evidence and seeking information from various sources.

There may be times when you are not really sure about what you want to pursue in your CAS efforts. In this case, the Investigation starts with you! Use this stage to find out what your interests and aspirations are; this will guide you towards potential CAS that you are more likely to enjoy and benefit from. As CAS is a discovery of self, others and communities that can assist you in finding your own place in the world, Investigation can assist you in exposing these discoveries. The short survey below can help you in this process.

ACTIVITY BOX

Part A – Investigating you!

What are your interests? What hobbies do you like, or would like to get involved in? What skills do you have, or would like to develop? Are there certain attributes of the IB learner profile (see Chapter 1, section 1.07) you would like to explore or enhance? What issues of public significance would you like to take action in addressing? What experiences could you do for CAS? What would you like to learn more about or become involved in? What barriers may exist in limiting your participation?

Part B – Investigating communities

The plural 'communities' is used here because there are different communities you could consider – the immediate local community, the broader local community, or a community interstate or overseas. When it comes to taking appropriate action in response to a global issue, it does not mean you need to look globally. It is wise to consider the adage 'think global, act local' here, as engaging locally is logistically more accessible, and may allow for a closer working relationship with that community.

How could you gather information about your chosen community? What issues does the community face? How could you get involved in addressing the issue? Are there any steps previously/presently undertaken to address this issue? Which organisations are involved in taking action to address the issue? Could you join others already taking steps in addressing this issue?

2

This commences once you have developed some ideas about what you may wish to pursue for your CAS.

- What resources do you need?
- Do you need to develop any skills or knowledge before you start participating?
- What will your SMART goals be?
- Are there any costs involved? Who could you approach to support you if required?

Global issue: issues of public significance or concern that manifest in local and worldwide contexts.

SMART goals: a set of criteria to follow so that you can help make your goals a reality. Goals should be Specific, Measurable, Attainable, Realistic and Timely.

Before you can proceed with preparing for your involvement, you need to become knowledgeable about the CAS experience you are about to undertake. If your CAS is in the area of Service, it is important that you investigate the issue you are addressing, how it affects the community you are aiming to work with, what has been done previously to address it, and what others are doing. This investigation not only adds to your capabilities in planning and implementing your CAS, but it may also change the direction of your intended work. For example, your investigation may lead you to conclude that it would be wise to join the work being done by others in your chosen area rather than starting up your own project.

For specific details about the use of the CAS stages in service-related projects, turn to Chapter 6.

Below is a list of global issues that may manifest in your local community. After you have done some research to develop your understanding of these issues, rank them with these two points in mind:

1   Which issues are you most interested in taking action on?
2   Which issues offer you the most opportunity to do something about them?

You could then consider your final ranking as an indication of which issues you could take action on as a part of your CAS.

- Climate change
- Communicable diseases
- Conflict resolution and prevention
- Deforestation
- Disadvantaged youth
- Elderly people
- Education for all
- Fisheries depletion
- Food security
- Gender inequality
- Human rights
- Immigrants
- Natural disaster mitigation
- Pollution
- Poverty
- Waste management
- Water deficits

Looking for ideas on possible global issues that you could take appropriate action on? The United Nations Millennium Development Goals (MDGs) could be a place to start. Though at the time of writing the deadline for reaching these goals – 2015 – was almost reached, the MDGs still offer a good starting point for exploring global issues. Refer to the reference list at the end of this chapter for details on the book *High Noon: 20 global problems, 20 years to solve them*, which could be another resource to help develop your understanding on global issues.

Figure 2.2 Millennium Development Goals
(www.un.org/millenniumgoals/)

Another aspect of the Investigation stage is considering what risks your involvement may pose for you. This is what is referred to as a 'risk assessment'. Let's look at this briefly.

Risk assessment

What risks might you be exposed to as a part of your CAS? As a part of your investigation, you could assist your CAS Coordinator by being involved in the following elements of risk assessment:

- considering the likelihood of risks occurring
- identifying the causes of risks
- outlining what steps could be taken to prevent risks
- detailing what action would be taken if risks did eventuate, including who to call and other emergency steps.

The level of risk involved, which is something your CAS Coordinator should determine, will guide the next steps in developing your risk assessment. The types of risk you may be exposed to include:

1 Risks posed by other people
   - Lack of experience or training
   - Lack of supervision
   - Aggression by others
   - Existing medical conditions
   - Poor communication
   - Not observing safety guidelines
   - Lack of preparation
   - Inappropriate behaviour
   - Non-observance of local laws

2 Risks posed by the environment
   - Weather conditions (heat, cold)
   - Transport/vehicles
   - Pollution
   - Equipment (e.g. machinery)
   - Exposure to chemicals
   - Animals
   - Electricity
   - Noise
   - Fire
   - Water

2

3   Risks posed by equipment
   •   Level of maintenance
   •   Faulty equipment
   •   Lack of safety equipment/clothing
   •   Appropriateness of equipment

2.02 Preparation

In its simplest terms, the Preparation stage involves thinking about what you are going to do, and how you are going to do it. During this stage you devise a plan for conducting the Action stage – this is commonly referred to as the 'action plan'. Things that you consider here include: the various tasks that need to be completed, the resources you will need to complete them, and a timeline of when things need to be completed and in what order. When your CAS involves collaborating with others, you also need to outline who needs to complete which tasks.

As you develop your ideas in preparing to act, you may need to go back to the Investigation stage to gather the information you require to improve your planning. The extent of your planning is very much dependent upon the nature of the CAS experience or project you are planning. Due to its duration and complexity, a CAS project will obviously require more time in order to prepare for your involvement in it, while some CAS experiences, such as learning the guitar, may simply involve scheduling lessons and setting a goal and date to reach this goal.

The Preparation stage also involves identifying the skills that would be necessary for you to participate in your CAS experience or project. Though the development of these skills may be a part of the next stage of CAS – the actual participation in the experience – it is important that you commence development of these skills, or in some cases become capable in them, before you start the Action stage. There may even be times when you need to complete some training or get professional support before you can start your participation. For example, if you were aiming to publish a magazine or run a half-marathon, you would benefit from some initial professional advice and training before starting your involvement. As with the degree of preparation required, the need to develop new skills is dependent upon the complexity of the CAS experience you are getting ready to undertake.

Figure 2.3 The Preparation stage involves thinking about what you are going to do and planning how you are going to do it.

The following activity may help you answer the question: Just how much planning do I need to do before I can take action?

Rank the following possible CAS experiences from least to most in regards to the approximate time you think is required to complete the Investigation/Preparation stages. See our responses below.

- Organising a charity concert
- Monthly hiking/trekking
- Web design/HTML code course
- Tennis lessons
- Member of the school basketball team
- Model UN club (Secretary of the club and Model UN participation)

2

The answers provided here could be challenged as they very much depend upon the exact nature of the CAS experiences listed, and the individual student who would be pursuing them. What they do provide is an indication of the difference in length of time required in these two stages of CAS. The purpose of this activity is to help you understand that the level of work in the initial CAS stages is dependent upon the nature of the CAS you are preparing to undertake.

6. Organising a charity concert
4. Monthly hiking/trekking 5. Model UN club (Secretary of the club and Model UN participation)
1. Tennis lessons 2. Member of the school basketball team 3. Web design/HTML code course

2.03 Action

This is the 'doing' part of CAS, where you implement the plans that you developed in the Preparation stage. It is the easiest of the five CAS stages to understand as it simply involves following the plans you have prepared. It does, however, require you to take the time to reflect as you participate, and refer back to your preparation notes to make sure you complete all the tasks you set yourself. As outlined in Chapter 3, reflecting is a key part of learning from our experiences, and it often influences our ongoing participation and future actions.

There are some cases where the Action stage may not necessarily follow the Investigation or Preparation stages, such as when your friend invites you to go with them for a rock-climbing course the next day, or where you have an opportunity to join the set-design team for the school production that is meeting that very evening. Wherever possible, though, it is best that you do the Investigation and Preparation that is required for a particular CAS experience. It is likely that you will get more out of your CAS if you are prepared for it.

Key point: It is recommended that CAS endeavours involve some kind of planning. At the very least, considering why you might get involved in a particular experience, what you will get out of it, and how it might fit into your busy schedule as a Diploma student, are worthy thoughts before signing up for a new experience!

Action plan: an outline of tasks that need to be completed in order to achieve a defined goal, who will complete them, and when they are to be completed by.

ACITIVY BOX

Complete the following action plan template to help you prepare for your CAS involvement. An excerpt from an action plan for organising a Speech Contest is provided below.

Main activity	Specific actions (What needs to be done?)	Who will be responsible?	Resources that will help	Date to be completed by

Main Activity	Specific actions (What needs to be done?)	Who will be responsible?	Resources that will help	Date to be completed by
Location logistics	1. Venue booking 2. Seating 3. Stage set up	1. Yani 2. Yani 3. Riana	Mr Richards	1. July 1st 2. October 10th 3. October 15th
Promotions	1. Media release 2. Poster 3. Website 4. eflyer	1. Ansu 2. Nigel 3. Nigel 4. Nigel	Ms Mather (text) Mr Kay (design) Examples of poster and eflyer	1. August 1st 2. August 1st 3. August 1st 4. August 1st
Speakers	1. Send invitations 2. Provide guidelines 3. Get speaker bios	1. Ansu 2. Ansu 3. Ryan	Check guidelines for other speech competitions Consult Mr Ahmad	1. September 10th 2. October 1st 3. October 1st
Sponsors	1. Develop sponsorship proposal 2. Send proposals, present to those interested 3. Gather logos for promotional material	1. Ryan 2. Ryan 3. Riana	Ms Mather (text) Sample sponsorship proposal	1. July 1st 2. July 5th 3. July 15th

2

Let's now look at a CAS Case Study that provides an example of some of the tasks conducted in the Investigation, Preparation and Action CAS stages of this CAS project.

CAS CASE STUDY

Cachorritos CAS Project. Unidad Educativa Particular Ecomundo, Guayaquil, Ecuador

This project is aimed at increasing concern for animal rights and developing community awareness about their role in animal welfare. The project name 'Cachorritos' was chosen because it represents a vulnerable animal. A part of the project, which was conceived at InterCAS, focused on working with institutions that support people with autism to use pets as a form of therapy.

> **InterCAS:** conferences held in various countries, especially in South America, which bring together students and CAS Coordinators from a large number of schools to learn about a particular theme for CAS and to share CAS experiences and achievements together.

Investigation

An initial Investigation focused on identifying the community's knowledge about animal welfare and animal rights. Following this, investigation included:

- evaluation of potential projects (financial and administrative feasibility) that can integrate pets as a part of community activities
- identification of groups and institutions that participate and influence improvement in the quality of animal life and explore opportunities for collaboration with our project
- evaluation of potential events, logistics and human resources requirements to undertake the project.

Preparation

The group made an analysis of the financial feasibility of the project, which involved making a budget and potential sources of income to fund the project. A scenario analysis was then created to identify opportunities and threats of the project implementation. Roles for group members were then assigned, with specific duties and responsibilities defined. The group also cooperated with the Ecuadorian IB School Association (ASECCBI) to prepare for InterCAS Ecuador 2014, where activities were delivered that involved the use of dogs in providing therapy to people with autism.

Action

The group was involved in a number of Action tasks, including:

- bimonthly coordination and follow-up meetings to design schedules, contact suppliers, strategic allies and sponsors, organise events and request permits from the school board of governors, parents and local authorities (as required)
- work in coordination with animals' adoption centres in several projects such as:
  - assisting foundations in finding families that would like to adopt homeless pets.
  - supporting the role of foundations in promoting, educating and creating community awareness about the rights of animals
  - working in cooperation with foundations in promoting care for animals and training facilities to pet owners
  - working in cooperation with Canoterapia Querataro to learn about the use of dogs in providing therapy to individuals with autism, Downs Syndrome, and people with special needs. In addition, we launched a pilot project to train dogs to assist people with special needs
- facilitating workshops on topics such as: caring, adoption and sterilisation of pets
- donation of food to an organisation that ran an animal rescue centre
- organisation and participation in the Ecomundo internal CAS Fair presenting the project to the school community
- participation in the InterCAS Ecuador 2014, where 20 schools from Ecuador were involved in activities to develop a sense of responsibility and consciousness about autism. Our specific focus included use of pets as a therapeutic tool.

2.04 Reflection

Reflection is an integral part of CAS. By reflecting upon our involvement in an event – before, during and after – we are in a position to learn more from our experiences. It can help us be aware of the thoughts and feelings we have as a result of our participation, to understand ourselves more, and to consider the motives behind our choices and the choices of others. Though the term 'CAS stages' implies that each phase is to be completed sequentially, it is best for reflection to occur throughout the CAS process. In this way, reflection can assist with preparing for participation, guide future actions, indicate that further investigation may be required and facilitate the demonstration of your engagement.

Chapter 3 provides further guidance that will help you benefit most from this important part of your CAS programme. Now let's look at the following CAS Snapshot, which provides us with an example of a student's reflection.

Key point: The CAS stages are not to be thought of as a cycle, or a step-by-step process. Going though the stages is not always sequential, and going back to a previous stage could be an important part of the process.

CAS SNAPSHOT

InterCAS Ecuador 2014, CAS reflection

The first national InterCAS was held in the city of Ambato, where the main point of this gathering was highlighting the importance of taking care of an autistic child. Over four days a number of activities were organised – hiking, fairs, intercultural events and service activities involving autistic children. As participants in InterCAS, we received new insights for understanding the unique world of an autistic child. During the service component we had the opportunity to be a part of different activities like: sensory, interaction, music, recreation and more.

There are several elements that can be drawn from this experience. Being able to talk and interact with people who have different concentration and understanding skills allowed me to adapt to their environment. It also led me to inquire about ways of supporting those with different needs in society, and also consider whose responsibility this is (all of ours!).

I gained a lot of admiration for the mothers who are dedicated to the ongoing care of their children, perhaps more than some communities or governments show. In the social sphere, we shared unique moments with young people from IB schools around the country. We shared ideas, listened to new views and reached consensus when we did not agree. We also forged lots of new friendships!

Sara, Unidad Educativa Particular Ecomundo. Guayaquil, Ecuador.

2.05 Demonstration

This stage involves sharing your CAS involvement with an audience, generally once your involvement in the CAS experience or project is at its end. The audience you choose, and how you present and celebrate your CAS, is up to you. You may write something for the school newsletter or school website, you may make a public display or a booklet, or you may present to your class, an assembly or to students at another school. You may choose to opt for a 'virtual' audience and use an online platform to showcase your CAS. The key here is not how you present, but the content of what you share and the process of gathering and sharing the key parts of your CAS experience/project.

It is worth considering how you may demonstrate your CAS experience during the earlier stages. Doing so may enable you to collect the documentation or capture moments on camera that you may wish to share. Thinking in advance about the best way to present the project might actually enrich the whole experience by sparking more ideas about your CAS participation.

The process of sharing your CAS with others in itself adds to your learning about your CAS involvement. Looking back at your participation – picking out the barriers you faced and how you overcame them, or the accomplishments you achieved and what helped you make them happen, and considering the most important things you gained from the experience – helps deepen the learning you take from it. Highlighting the important reflections that reveal different aspects of learning, together with the evidence of achieving those learning

2

outcomes, is also a part of this process. Communicating these to an audience also helps to deepen understanding of what you gained from your CAS engagement, especially when there is dialogue about your CAS between you and the audience. In a sense, the Demonstration stage serves as a summary reflection of your CAS experience or project.

Figure 2.4 Sharing your CAS with others through a public presentation.

2.06 Examples of the CAS stages

Now let us look at examples of the CAS stages in each of the three strands of CAS – Creativity, Activity and Service.

CAS CASE STUDY

The CAS stages in Creativity

Investigation

In starting this stage, I already knew that I wanted to get involved in something to do with theatre. I enjoyed drama in my junior high school, and was disappointed that I could not include Theatre in my Diploma Programme subjects. I met the theatre teacher at my school to discuss my options, and also did some research online about the drama schools/clubs in the areas I could travel to. After considering my options, I decided to join a course called 'Acting antics' – a weekly class providing acting lessons.

Preparation

Anybody could join this group, regardless of acting ability or experience, so I did not have to do any training before I got involved. As the course was already set out, with set weekly lessons and a final performance, I did not have to plan much. I organised transport arrangements with my parents – this involved finding out about public transport options. In the final stages of the Action stage, I had to return to my planning so that I could make arrangements to attend the additional rehearsals for the final performance.

Action

I attended weekly sessions for three months. In the final few weeks, I also attended rehearsals, and practised at home.

Reflection

I had some photos of the final performance, as well as some video clips, which I added to my CAS portfolio along with some brief written reflections related to being challenged and learning new skills. During the early stages of the experience I recorded a short clip that focused on how I thought I would benefit from the increased confidence in public speaking the course was giving me, and shared it with my CAS Advisor.

2

Figure 2.5 A performance of 'Two Jagged Lines' at Discovery College.

> **Key point:** In most cases, but not all, the first stage of involvement in CAS would be the Investigation stage. For CAS projects, or CAS experiences of a more significant duration, commencing with the Investigation stage becomes more important. Regardless of the length of the experience or project, reflection should be ongoing, taking place as required in the various CAS stages rather than taking place only after your engagement has finished.

Demonstration

The final performance was a showcase of what I gained from the course. After some encouragement from my CAS Advisor, I also performed a monologue from a scene to my homeroom at school, where I answered a few questions from the CAS Advisor about some of the key things I gained from my experience.

CAS CASE STUDY

The CAS stages in Activity

Investigation

I wanted to do something that would help me with my general fitness. I never really liked sports, but felt I needed to do some type of physical activity. CAS provided me with the push I needed to get started in something. After speaking with some friends and reading some fitness magazines in the library, I narrowed my options down to attending yoga or Pilates classes at the local gym, getting a personal trainer or following a training programme that I could find online. When I looked into it further, I found out some of the costs involved. This ruled out most options – I was left with following an online programme.

I spoke to my former PE teacher for advice. She gave me some good ideas, including how important it was that I got some support on what programme to follow and how to do some of the exercises properly. I did some research online, and I found some good resources including some cool apps that seemed comprehensive and easy to follow. I went back to my old PE teacher, who graciously looked at the apps, helped me select one to follow and showed me the proper way to do the exercises.

Key point: Important aspects of your CAS programme are personal engagement, choice and enjoyment of CAS experiences. You should plan your engagement so that CAS experiences are not only beneficial but also enjoyable.

Preparation

Following advice from my PE teacher, I started just by jogging three times a week for two weeks, increasing the intensity, just so my body was not so shocked when I started my programme after not exercising for a while. I set some goals – to be able to do 10 push-ups, 20 sit-ups and 20 bench hops within 70 seconds after eight weeks of training. I selected an appropriate programme from the app, with support from my PE teacher, and set it out for eight weeks of training. I only needed to get a few resources – gym clothes and a new pair of trainers!

Action

I trained three times a week. At first it was difficult to motivate myself, but once I started using music to train to, I found it easier. The app was easy to use and linked to my calendar, so I was reminded about training.

Reflection

I kept a weekly training journal, where I added some thoughts and feelings about how my training was going each week. Some of the key points that I noted here linked to the CAS learning outcomes about own strengths and areas for growth, as I realised how much I enjoyed becoming fitter and stronger, and how this improved my self-esteem and confidence. In the summary reflection for the CAS portfolio I also highlighted that doing the training became a stress release for me, that in training I could forget about my studies and other worries.

Demonstration

My PE teacher asked me to speak to one of her classes that was studying a fitness unit. It was just for a few minutes to talk about how important goals were, and also how I motivated myself to achieve them. I uploaded what I prepared to say to them to my CAS portfolio. Though it wasn't formally sharing what I achieved in this CAS experience, I did 10 push-ups in the cafeteria to impress my friends! While it was a bit of a joke, I was really proud that I could do this.

CAS portfolio: a collection of your CAS planning, reflections, and evidence of CAS involvement and achievements.

SPOTLIGHT ON ... EVIDENCE

Showing evidence of the learning outcomes is a key part of CAS. In many cases the new skills you develop, or start the development of, in the Preparation stage of CAS could act as evidence of achievement in the CAS learning outcome: to 'demonstrate that challenges have been undertaken, developing new skills in the process'. You should therefore keep some evidence of the development of these skills in your CAS portfolio. Evidence of achievement in the CAS learning outcomes and of your participation in CAS is to be kept in your CAS portfolio. Your school may require you to present your CAS portfolio in a certain way, or you may have a choice about how you present it. Whatever the method, the portfolio is a mandated way for you to *demonstrate* evidence of what you have done, learnt and gained from your CAS programme.

CAS CASE STUDY

The CAS stages in Service

Investigation

As I was not sure what I wanted to do in regards to Service, my CAS Advisor asked a few students and me to complete a survey that asked about our interests, and what issues in our community we would consider getting involved in doing something about. From answering the questions and talking with the others in activities led by our CAS Advisor, Jonah and I both showed interest in doing something to support the natural environment. We discussed some different ideas, including recycling and saving energy. We then did some online research, and spoke to our parents about it. Jonah's mum had a friend who used to work with an organisation that promoted environmental sustainability, so we emailed her. She suggested that we look into how the things we consume and buy have an impact on the environment; she said that it might be possible to make a big difference to our own global footprint simply by changing what we buy. She suggested we do some research about ethical consumerism. We did, and found some details on fair trade, which we then focused on. We started collecting some information about what fair trade was, and what fair trade products were available to us. We visited a fair trade store, and were able to ask the owner a few questions about fair trade. We also collected some data from the supermarket, looking at different fair trade products available. We asked students in our classes about what they knew about fair trade, which generally was not that much; they rarely bought fair trade products. That is when we thought it would be great if fair trade products could be available in the school cafeteria, and we could help promote and create awareness about fair trade. We made an appointment with the cafeteria manager, who was supportive of our ideas. Together we brainstormed some ideas, and identified some further information we needed about product costs and supplies. We emailed the owner of the fair trade shop who was able to provide the answers we needed. We then confirmed our aims – to inform the school community about fair trade (via a website, information displays and school assemblies), promote them as an ethical product, and have some fair trade products sold in the school canteen (chocolates, dried fruit, nuts, muffins, coffee).

Preparation

We created an action plan that outlined our roles, resources we required and dates that we set to finish tasks by. In creating this plan, we realised that neither of us had any experience in website design, so before we started our website, we both did an online course as well as using YouTube clips to learn how to use HTML software. Our school IT teacher also helped us here. It became clear to us that we did not know enough about sales, but luckily the canteen manager was controlling those parts of the project.

Action

We set up the website first, and then created our display. We manned this in front of the school cafeteria each lunchtime for a week before the goods went on sale at the cafeteria. We also spoke to different year level assemblies, giving a 10-minute presentation about fair trade and encouraging students to buy fair trade. After doing this we realised we needed to do something to inform staff, so we went back to our action plan and added some details to inform staff (we spoke at a staff meeting). We created some promotional material for the fair trade goods on sale in the cafeteria, and on the day they first went on sale we gave out some free taste-testing samples.

Key point: In CAS, reflection should not be seen as an obligation but a purposeful part of learning.

Reflection

I provided my CAS Advisor with a few written reflections that I made during my involvement, which I also added to my CAS portfolio. Here is a written reflection I added in the early stages of involvement – 'I'm getting really excited about this. Just met with the cafeteria manager and she was really supportive about our ideas, in fact she even had some ideas to build on our thoughts. I'm actually a bit surprised about how keen I am to get the next steps done.'

A reflection from the later stages of the project – 'Jonah and I have worked well together. Though we have had a few issues, mainly around communication, we have done a good job. I think a key part to this was that we clearly assigned tasks in our plans, and that we discussed these regularly. I like the way that Jonah was honest when he thought that things were not good enough, but in a way that didn't hurt my feelings.'

Demonstration

Our website demonstrated what we accomplished – the information about fair trade, products available in local supermarkets and the fair trade shop, and the promotion of goods in our cafeteria. We also included a film of the presentations we gave at school assemblies, and updated it to show sales figures of the fair trade products at the cafeteria.

2.07 Review of Chapter 2

1   Which stage of the CAS stages framework do you think would be most difficult?

2   In what ways have you used the stages outlined in this chapter in other aspects of your academic studies? What about in your personal life?

3   Do you think that one stage of this framework is more important than others? Why?

2.08 A summary of this chapter

In this chapter we have:

1   Explored the CAS stages:
    • Investigation
    • Preparation
    • Action
    • Reflection
    • Demonstration.

2   Looked at examples of the use of the CAS stages in:
    • Creativity
    • Activity
    • Service.

Reflection

Reflection is the key to learning from experiential education, and that is why it is emphasised in this book.

Experiential education: a philosophy of education where students become actively involved in the learning process. It is learning by action and reflecting on that action.

As already highlighted in Chapter 2, reflection is a key part of CAS. Reflection is the way in which we understand what has happened and convert an experience into learning. Some may go as far as saying that without reflection, you will not actually learn from your CAS experiences!

Though an integral part of CAS, reflection is not always well understood. Reflection can be perceived as a challenging task for students and teachers. Everybody, in every IB subject, talks about meaningful reflection – reflective skills; developing and utilising powers of reflection; critical and creative thinking; reflective practice, and so on. And let's not forget that being reflective is also one of the IB learner profile attributes! Despite all this, reflection is not always clearly taught, which may lead to confusion and misunderstanding.

This chapter aims to highlight what reflection in CAS should involve. We will first look at what reflection actually is in section 3.01, and how we can develop reflective skills to gain more from our CAS experiences in section 3.02. We will consider ways of deepening our reflections in section 3.03 and look at the different forms of reflection in section 3.04, including how reflection in other areas of the Diploma Programme core (CAS, TOK and extended essay (EE)), see section 3.05, can benefit your reflections in CAS, and *vice versa*.

If you follow the advice in this chapter you will find that reflection is not too difficult nor too time-consuming, but something that can help you to understand your experiences and learn from them.

Let's start by asking the right questions.

- Why are we expected to reflect?
- What are the main characteristics of the reflection process?
- What does a significant CAS reflection mean?
- How can we undertake a meaningful reflection process?

3

3.01 Understanding reflection: helping to make sense of reflection

When looking at the reflection process, it is worth clarifying what reflection is not.

Reflection is far from being a prescribed task. It is not just a requirement to fulfil obligations or expectations; it is not something to be completed just to please someone else. Nor should reflection be forced during a predetermined time established by others.

It is not something submitted for assessment – although it could be argued that there can be differences in the quality of a reflection, it is not something that can be right or wrong. And it may not even have to be written down.

Definition of reflection

'Experience is not what happens to you; it's what you do with what happens to you.' *(Aldous Huxley)*

The power of reflection is a human capacity that needs to be developed; it implies higher cognitive processes which enable us to become more acutely aware of what happens to us – it is the way to make us masters of our own lives!

Reflection is a dynamic means of self-discovery. It leads to personal and interpersonal growth, and helps us to develop to our fullest, holistic potential: psychologically, emotionally, socially, ethically, spiritually as well as cognitively.

Reflection can help you to:

- better understand your strengths, weaknesses and areas for improvement
- develop your decision-making and problem-solving skills
- identify your values and beliefs, and those of others
- consider and act upon feedback
- make more sense of your experiences, and how they may shape your actions
- acknowledge and challenge assumptions on which you base your ideas, choices, feelings and actions
- apply learning from one situation to another
- make links between CAS experiences and other IB subjects and components
- better understand yourself, and those you interact with.

Life is a journey of learning, and this learning process is meaningfully enhanced when we get in touch with our life-situations and experiences.

Critical reflection is what transforms life-situations into learning experiences

We learn most from what we actively experience, and it is from real-life experiences that true and lasting changes of attitude are achieved. Those changes involve many different thoughts, feelings and behaviours.

I hear and I forget.
I see and I remember.
I do and I understand.   *(Confucius)*

When going through the experiential learning process, we discover the combination of components that make up meaningful learning (concepts, criteria and feelings); we are actively involved in the process, becoming the force behind our own learning.

According to Carl Rogers, learning is experiential when it includes 'The whole person, both in feelings and in cognitive aspects' and when it 'makes a difference in the behaviour, the attitudes, perhaps even the personality of the learner'.

(Rogers and Freiberg, 1994:36)

3

Reflection is situated learning, because it helps give meaning to what is experienced, and thus what is learned. It is an important part of being a critical thinker, and it is a goal for many of your teachers that you should habitually reflect. In this way it becomes a part of the learning you take from daily life, and is part of your preparation to face adult life in an ever-changing world, full of uncertainties. We can learn to act in the present, looking ahead into the future.

Key point: CAS is learning by action and reflecting on that action.

Some contributions from a psychological perspective

The reflection process involves cognitive activity in each cerebral hemisphere: the emotional elements in the right hemisphere, and the rational elements in the left.

As you may discuss in your TOK classes, the process of absorbing knowledge starts from an outside stimulus, which in turn produces a physical stimulus within the nervous system. The right cerebral hemisphere, which is connected with arts, intuition, creativity and emotional responses, receives a message that is then transmitted to the left hemisphere, which is in charge of reasoning, abstraction and conceptualisation. From there, knowledge is formulated, and it can be stored, remembered and applied to other life situations.

Experiential learning enables us to put learning in context, giving meaning to specific situations that take place during human interactions. Experiential learning has the potential to involve every part of our human dimension: biological, cognitive, emotional, ethical, spiritual and socio-cultural processes. It involves the whole person, and it is through the process of reflection that we can develop our awareness of these dimensions, and deepen our understanding of the impact of our involvement.

3.02 Reflection at each of the CAS stages

As outlined in Chapter 2, reflection should be an ongoing process, taking place over time. It should both influence, and be influenced by, our decisions and actions at each of the CAS stages.

Reflection before: Investigation and Preparation

In these first two stages, you will consider how you might use prior learning in new contexts. It is the moment of inquiry, and provides you with opportunities to develop decision-making skills. See the CAS Stages Framework, section 2.1.

All three elements of the Diploma Programme core (CAS, TOK and EE) should be grounded in three coherent aims, including to support, and to be supported by, the academic disciplines so as to be informed and enriched by them. You may discover information, methods of analysis, great ideas and proposals for significant CAS experiences in other IB Diploma Programme subjects. TOK may provide interesting questions to ask yourself before deciding to take any action.

CAS Proposal 1
Berliner Tafel

In this example you can see how students carried out a CAS experience inspired by an economics lesson.

'We wanted to go to work in the Berliner Tafel for a week. The Tafel collects food donations from supermarkets in Berlin and redistributes them to needy people and families. Five of us decided to do this because we were interested in helping less privileged people in Berlin – a subject we had discussed in an economics lesson. Our preparation involved:

a researching organisations on the internet and deciding which one we wanted to help

b contacting the Tafel and getting them to accept us for help during our summer holidays c organising accommodation in Berlin

d organising transport to and from Berlin

e budgeting for the trip.

This meant that we had to assign roles for people, organise meetings and set deadlines.'

CAS Proposal 2
Book circle

In this example you can see a CAS experience driven by student passion, and related to an academic subject.

'My passion is to read, read and read. I read books, journals, essays, newspapers, magazines, anything. I am taking Language A: English HL and that taught me how to explore literature more deeply, and now I want to use these skills to develop a book circle. I think this would be creative.

'I am starting this circle from scratch, so that means I will demonstrate how to initiate and plan a CAS experience. I am aiming to meet at least once every two weeks for, hopefully, one year to show my commitment and perseverance. I will plan some special events during the year with other participants.'

Reflection during the experience: Action

This is the time to reflect on your actions, develop problem-solving skills by considering possible alternatives and courses of action, understand what you are doing well and where you need to improve.

CAS SNAPSHOT

These examples show how reflection during a CAS project led students to change the course of actions to meet other people's needs and characteristics.

1 'We had signed up with the Red Cross to work with people in the home for the blind, where most of the occupants were elderly women. After looking at the various activities that we could help with, we decided that we would go every Wednesday afternoon to read to the ladies. However, after our first visit, when we read them a

love story that ended tragically, we realised that we had made a terrible mistake – many of the old ladies were in tears and left us shaking their heads. So we had to find out what the problem had been. They told us that they did not want to hear anything that ended depressingly and tragically. So we had to think very carefully about our choice of stories. Fortunately, we had both been reading the novel *Clochemerle*, which is about a dispute in a small French village over the installation of a urinal in the main square.

'This novel has many ridiculous and ironic parts and we decided to read some chapters in the form of a serial. The changes we made required quite a bit of thought. To make it more interesting we decided to take the roles of the main characters in our readings. This change in material and presentation was really important and the ladies looked forward to our visit even more.'

2   'After considering different opportunities, we decided to teach English lessons to primary school children in a state school. In our country, children going to public schools have little chance to develop English language skills. At the beginning, our lessons were writing- and reading-based. As days went by, we realised that our young students didn't enjoy the lessons and they looked bored, showing no interest at all. On the advice of our English teacher, we decided to change our strategy and teach English language through play. It worked! Every week children were waiting for us, eager to play and learn.'

Reflection after the experience: Demonstration and communication

Now is the time for self-evaluation; to step back from your experience and discuss your ideas and questions, share your changing perspectives, draw conclusions and think about the learning outcomes that you have achieved.

You can demonstrate and communicate the achievement of the seven CAS learning outcomes by reflecting on your CAS experiences included in your CAS portfolio.

For more details about how to reflect on CAS learning outcomes, see Chapter 10.

3

> **CAS experience:** a specific event in which the student engages with one or more of the three CAS strands. It can be a single event or may be an extended series of events.
>
> *CAS Guide* (2015), page 14, IBO

CAS SNAPSHOT

In the examples below you can find different moments of reflection during CAS experiences.

1. 'We gave a presentation about our cycling trip along the River Elbe from Magdeburg to Hamburg. This is a summary of a power point demonstration we showed.

   'Our original plan had been to do this in two weeks and camp out along the way. We managed to get to Magdeburg with our bikes after a seven-hour train trip and several changes. The first problem was in Magdeburg, where we had arranged to stay in a B & B and they did not have a secure place to put our bikes, so we had to take off the wheels and lock the frames to a tree in the back yard. This delayed our start by nearly half a day. We had planned to cycle 100 km that first day, but the temperature climbed to over 35° and this meant that we did not reach our planned destination until 10 p.m. We were both exhausted and asked a farmer if we could pitch our tent in his front yard. However, it took us an hour to erect our tent and it later collapsed, so we did not get much sleep. This was the start of a major argument that lasted for two days!

   'This taught us the importance of starting early and not being quite so ambitious, and also that we needed to listen to each other better. This proved to be important as the trip went on. Hans suggested that we take an alternative route one day because it would save us a further 25 km on a long day. After the first couple of days we had managed to get over saddle-soreness. The only other drama we had was getting a puncture one day, and we discovered that our puncture kit no longer had usable patches for the inner tube. So I had to cycle 20 km to the nearest town with the inner tube to get it fixed. That took ages to get sorted out and when I returned there were a group of fellow cyclists there offering help. It made us realise how kind people can be.

   'It was a great feeling to reach the Alder in Hamburg and realise how far we had travelled. The next trip planned is along the Canal du Midi from Toulouse to Narbonne.'

2 'Indoor drumline or winter drumline is the equivalent of an off-season sport, but for marching percussion. We learn a marching show that only uses percussion instruments including a full battery (snare drum, bass drum, quads, toms) and front ensemble (marimba, vibraphone, xylophone, bells, synthesizer and other electronics). We perform in gyms and use a 'floor' (a painted or coloured tarp used to protect the gym floor). Our shows have themes with costumes and acting integrated.

'When our school first started doing indoor drumline during the off season, I didn't really know what to expect. However, after our first competitive season, I learned how exhausting and time-consuming six hours of rehearsal a week can be, but how worthwhile it is when you walk off the floor with your friends, breathless after a great performance. I like indoor drumline because it focuses only on percussion and is mentally and physically difficult. We play a piece of music, in a dynamic and extremely musical way, while acting out a story with our bodies at the same time; it's like musical theatre on steroids. This was the first time I had really put a lot of time and physical effort into something, and it completely paid off at the end.'

Figure 3.1 Students in action.

Key point: Reflection should be an ongoing process, taking place over time. It should both influence and be influenced by our decisions and actions at each of the CAS stages.

3

The school year begins at school 'Z' and the teachers meet to coordinate activities. The CAS Coordinator suggests that he would like to coordinate a project related to other subject areas.

An English teacher says that this year she will be working on immunisation and suggests that students could design posters as part of a campaign to promote immunisation. Then they could take them to public hospital 'M' which specialises in mother-and-baby care for low-income patients. For a whole month, students work on creating the posters, which they plan to hang on the walls of the waiting rooms and along the corridors.

When everything is almost ready, the students schedule a visit to the hospital to deliver their work, which they see as a valuable contribution. They have devoted a lot of time and effort to this project, spent money on expensive materials, applied techniques they have learned in art classes and also put into practice communication skills in a second language. They are happy!

They arrive at the hospital and ask for an interview with the Director. He is very kind and listens attentively. They tell him about the IB Diploma, CAS and their willingness to provide a service to the community.

The Director looks carefully at the posters and congratulates them on their work. 'The posters look great! Well done! But ... mums who come to this hospital do not speak English.'

Imagine you are one of the students involved.

1 Analyse and evaluate this CAS experience according to the steps described in Section 3.02.
   • Reflection before the experience: Investigation and Preparation
   • Reflection during the experience: Action
   • Reflection after the experience: Demonstration

You can choose the form of reflection you like the most: be creative!

2 Conclusion: What steps would you take to avoid this happening with your own CAS project?

3.03 Deepening the reflection process

What are the main characteristics of reflection?

The reflection process should be thoughtfully constructed, and should challenge and guide you in developing critical thinking about your experiences.

- It is not a natural or innate process – we need to learn how to be reflective. Hopefully your CAS Coordinator or CAS adviser will help you to get the most of your CAS experiences.
- You need to feel safe when sharing your thoughts, feelings and conclusions.
- Reflection activities should lead to a clear goal. They should be meaningful and recognised as a personal choice.
- Purposeful reflection is about quality rather than quantity.
- You are encouraged to choose personal and enjoyable forms of reflection based on your own preference.
- You should choose the appropriate moment, select the method and decide on the amount of time needed. A key goal is for you to develop autonomy and become independently reflective.

Key point: The power of reflection needs to be developed. It should not be assumed that it comes naturally.

How reflection transforms CAS into a true learning experience

Reflection is what enables you to think critically about your experiences and to learn independently.

When you reflect on your experiences, you think, and express your thoughts and feelings in different forms (such as writing, singing, dancing, drawing). You relate your experiences to other things happening in your life. You become aware of your feelings and you look ahead. You share your experiences with other people. In short, reflection

3

is what enables you to learn during and from experiences. Learning takes place through a combination of theory and practise, thought and action, observation and interaction.

What are the different parts of the reflection process?

Here are some ideas to work through, with questions to guide you:

- **Describing the situations**: What has happened? What is happening?

- **Analysing them and unwrapping the experience. Each experience may have emphasis on different parts of your personality and contribute in different ways**: How have we (I) felt, or how do we (I) feel now? How do we (I) think others have felt? What were the activities carried out? What abilities and attitudes were put into action by us (me) and others? Why have we (I) acted this way? What did we (I) expect to accomplish by this experience? Who have we (I) worked with?

- **Evaluating situations and making sense of what happened**: What have been the outcomes of the experience? For us (me) and for everyone involved? For the environment? Have we (I) achieved our (my) objectives? What difficulties did we (I) encounter? How and what did we (I) do to overcome them? What else could we (I) have done differently?

- **Drawing conclusions and learning achieved**: What did we (I) learn from this experience? Which of the IB learner profile attributes did we (I) develop? Were we (was I) able to build or develop any good? For us (me), for others, for the community?

- **Changing perspectives, generating ideas, asking questions**: How did our (my) decisions impact on others' lives? What are the consequences of our (my) decisions and actions for us (me), others and the environment? What did we (I) discover about ourselves (myself), others, the community? Have we (I) changed our (my) perspectives? In what way?

- **Planning further actions and looking ahead**: How can we (I) apply what we (I) have learnt in other life situations?

This is not a linear process; these are moments that make up a whole reflection process. You can go through the different moments in different stages.

Linear process: a process that progresses straight from one stage to another, with a starting point and an ending point.

The reflective cycle in Figure 3.2 captures the main points of what has been explained.

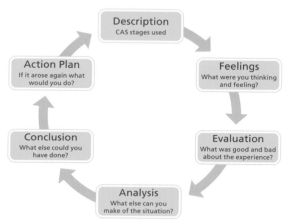

Figure 3.2 The reflective cycle. (from *Learning by Doing* by Graham Gibbs)

There are many ways to represent and carry out a reflection process. What matters is that you find your own style and follow the process at your own pace.

It is up to you! Be confident and feel free to deepen and express what you have lived.

Figure 3.3 Reflective attitude

3

3.04 Different types of reflection

Reflection can be carried out in countless forms. You should be able
to identify ways of expression that you find enjoyable, and which are a
good fit with the nature of the experience and your personal learning
style. You can consider using any of the following forms:

- Online: websites, blogs and other social media, apps, Powerpoint
  presentations
- On paper: drawing, creating a poster, letter, chart or scrapbook
- Dramatic or visual: a dramatic performance, video, audio, a verbal
  presentation, a song, poem, comic strip, photography, a dance.

You can find greater value and purpose when you apply your own
interests, skills and talents when reflecting. You discover that reflection
can be internal and private, or external and shared, done in groups or
individually.

Experiential learning is a personal process, where dialogue, exchange of
ideas and communication with others are essential. When you learn, you
become the owner of the experience and you are able to communicate
it to others. Learning results from the experience reflected and shared.

Below you can find some tips that can help you to systematise the
experiences in order to get the most out of them.

- Enquiring: What do we want to know about our experience? We
  need to set up guiding questions such as outcomes, difficulties and
  ways of overcoming them.
- Going through the experience: What have you experienced?
- Conceptualising: Which are the main concepts related to the
  experience?

- Developing emotional literacy: How did I feel in that experience?
- Drawing conclusions: What have I learnt from this?
- Socialising: Communicating and sharing experiences with others.

Key point: Reflection can be carried out in countless forms.

3.05 Developing the power of reflection

CAS and TOK

Developing critical reflection skills is a joint area between CAS and TOK.

CAS is a way of building knowledge from life situations. It is in that way that CAS is intimately related to TOK.

TOK encourages students to step back from the acquisition of knowledge and think critically about how that knowledge has been acquired.

In carrying out the critical reflection on a CAS experience, you can be guided by using each of the ways of knowing (WOKs).

Ways of knowing (WOK): the TOK course identifies eight specific WOKs. They are: language, sense perception, emotion, reason, imagination, faith, intuition, and memory.   *TOK Guide* (2013), page 8, IBO

CAS reflections go through a process including:

- a real–life situation
- our perception of the situation
- our emotional reaction to the situation
- use of reason to make sense of the situation
- language to express our feelings.

3

You may look at some aspects of the areas of knowledge as a means of framing your own set of values. CAS then can provide the experience of the world that enhances your knowledge of it.

For further development on CAS and TOK ways of knowing see Chapter 5, CAS, TOK and the extended essay.

Areas of knowledge (AOK): these are specific branches of knowledge, each of which has a distinct nature and uses different methods of gaining knowledge. TOK distinguishes between eight areas of knowledge: mathematics, the natural sciences, the human sciences, the arts, history, ethics, religious knowledge systems, and indigenous knowledge systems.
TOK Guide (2013), page 8, IBO

Key point: Developing critical reflection skills is a joint area between CAS and TOK.

CAS and the extended essay

The aims of the extended essay are to develop:

• research and communication skills
• creative and critical thinking skills.

Both aims are strongly related to CAS experiences. You can apply these skills throughout the CAS stages, particularly in the different moments of reflection.

Group reflections

Your reflection process can be significantly enhanced by group reflection with your peers. Communicating your thoughts, feelings and values enables you to discover shared insights and other points of view. For more ideas on group reflection activities you can go to section 6.01.

CAS SNAPSHOT

'Our group was bored of writing the same old reflections, so we decided to make a bit of a game of it. We took our reflection questions and made cards out of them. Then we all sat together and one at time we took a card and had to answer it as best we could. Anyone could then add to the answer if they wanted to, or agree or even disagree. We had great fun remembering all the things we had done and just how much we had achieved. Having achieved so much together it made perfect sense to reflect on it together. The questions helped us link our answer to the learning outcomes and – the best bit – our teacher videoed it and added it to our CAS portfolios for us. CAS reflection completed, and monitored, all in a fun lunchtime full of laughter and recollection.'

Key point: The reflection process can be significantly enhanced by sharing your experiences with others.

3

3.06 Review of Chapter 3

1   What for you are the most significant points of this chapter?

2   Which stage in the reflection process do you think would be most difficult to undertake, and why?

3   In what ways have you developed critical reflection skills in other aspects of your academic studies? What about in your personal life?

3.07 A summary of this chapter

In this chapter we have:

- Addressed a definition of reflection
- Explored some contributions from a psychological perspective
- Examined reflection at each of the CAS stages
- Looked at deepening the reflection process
- Developed ideas on what a reflection process is all about
- Explored different types of reflection
- Looked at developing powers of reflection by linking CAS reflection with TOK and EE as well as encouraging group reflections
- Looked at some examples of students' reflections and case studies.

CAS and service learning

4

Service is often considered the most transforming element of CAS. This is not to underplay the power of the other strands and their potential for meaningful impacts on students; one can easily see the significance of a student completing a half-marathon after months of training, or in playing on stage in a band after just learning to play the drums. There is, however, something to be said about the opportunities that service offers Diploma students.

Strands: refers to the three areas of CAS that gives this programme its name – Creativity, Activity, Service. All CAS experiences must fall within one of the three strands.

The service strand in CAS allows for the development of international mindedness, global citizenship and the attributes of the learner profile. In engaging yourself in service you can be an agent of change, doing something meaningful for society while developing as an individual.

This chapter will focus on helping you understand your role in service learning, to encourage you to look for opportunities to use and enhance your academic skills and knowledge in your CAS, and provide some examples of service learning in CAS. We will start by looking at service itself, and the various ways you could contribute meaningfully to your community. We will then explore the idea of service learning and how it applies to your CAS, and consider opportunities for service learning in the Diploma curriculum.

4.01 Service: Ways of engaging with the community

Service: the act of doing something for the benefit of others or for the greater good. Defined in *CAS Guide* (2015) as 'Collaborative and reciprocal engagement with the community in response to an authentic need'.

The service strand in CAS has evolved to be more than just helping others. In approaching your service, you should view it as an opportunity to work with others for mutual benefit, and to be an active citizen, aware of your responsibilities towards others.

Service involves a large spectrum of action taken with the aim of the improvement of the community. During your service, you could develop an awareness of, and subsequently change, your personal lifestyle choices, or you may become a public advocate, campaigning for change on a chosen issue. Whatever your service experience, the important thing is that it must aim to meet an identified need.

Key point: You are a member of a number of different communities – your school community, your local district or township, your national community and the global community, to name a few. When considering working with others, there are many different groups to engage with, but do keep in mind that the further away the community is, the more difficult it may be to work with them!

Before we explore service further, complete the questions in the activity box to think about what service means to you.

ACTIVITY BOX

1 What categories of service are you aware of? Do you think that some are more important than others?

2 Some may say that they do not like the term 'service' as used in the context of CAS because it provides for a power hierarchy. Under what circumstances do you think this is true? What are some other terms that you think would be appropriate?

Service, also referred to as community service, taking action, community outreach or civic engagement, should be approached in a way that respects the rights and dignity of the target community. When approached in a way that does not include all parties in the designing and implementing of plans, not only are desired outcomes rarely achieved, but the process can also contribute to a hierarchy of power. Despite the best intentions, such cases result in those offering the service as being seen, or even considering themselves, in a more socially privileged position than the recipients of the service. Later in this chapter we will outline what steps you can take to ensure that your service acts in the essence of reciprocity and respectful relationships.

4

> **Reciprocity:** in the context of service in CAS, the process where both parties in a service setting gain positively from the experience.

Let's now take a look at the different types of service you could get involved in as a part of your CAS.

4.02 Types of service

The *CAS Guide* outlines four types of service. While there is no stipulation about which type you should choose, nor about which one is more important, you should aim to include some direct service in your CAS programme because of the opportunity it offers to collaborate directly with those targeted by the service.

Direct service

This is where you directly engage with the people, environment or animals that form the target group. A benefit of this type of service is that you are better able to establish relationships with those you are working with, and can directly observe your impact. Examples of this face-to-face involvement include teaching literacy skills to a minority group, tree planting as a part of forest restoration or working in an elderly centre.

Figure 4.1   Direct service: planting trees at the InterCAS in Peru.

Indirect service

In this type of service, you participate with the recipients but are not in direct contact. It is important to highlight here that even though you may not directly see the community you are supporting, you will need to communicate with them so that your actions are aimed at an identified need and you are able to evaluate your actions to see if they are meeting your desired goals. The benefit of indirect service is that you may still be able to take action to support others despite transportation or access issues. Examples of indirect service include developing learning resources to be used by others, leading a computer skills project for the elderly, creating promotional material for an NGO or running an awareness campaign in your school for a local animal shelter.

NGO: Non-government organisation, also referred to as non-profit, is a community group not a part of government or for-profit business sectors. NGOs may provide you with a community partner for CAS service activities.

Advocacy

In this type of service you become an advocate for a particular organisation or cause in an attempt to change people's ideas, understanding and behaviours surrounding a particular global issue. This type of service provides obvious opportunities to engage yourself in addressing an issue of global significance – one of the seven CAS learning outcomes. You could conduct this type of service in your school, local community or even in an online environment. Examples of advocacy include campaigning for awareness about human rights abuses, speaking up in the community to prevent a planned development in a local wetland or becoming an ambassador for a regional NGO aiming to support migrant workers.

Figure 4.2 Young people demonstrating as a part of an environmental campaign.

4 Research

As the name implies, this type of service would involve you conducting research to report in some way on a significant topic, with the aim of your research informing and affecting guidelines, positions and ideas. The research would involve you collecting, analysing and synthesising information from various sources, and putting this together in some form of written, visual or oral report. Similar to advocacy, you could conduct this type of service in your school, local community or even in an online environment. A benefit of this type of service is that it can be done at a distance from the topic you are researching, as long as you have access to primary and secondary sources of information. The research you conduct may also lead you to take action on the particular topic of your research, providing an opportunity for engagement in one of the above-mentioned types of service. Examples of research include developing a report on the plight of low-paid migrant workers, conducting a survey of the school community in regards to a particular policy or investigating sources of marine litter in the local area.

Thinking about the types of service listed here, is there a certain type that you are more interested in? Are there more opportunities in your local community for a certain type of service? Is there a particular type of service you think would be more difficult? Why might you think this?

ACTIVITY BOX

Of the four types of service listed above, which type would the following experiences fit into?

- Organising/participating in a number of beach clean-ups
- Water-testing in a local wetland over a period of time
- Holding weekly craft sessions at an elderly centre
- Being a peer mediator in your school's peer-mentoring programme
- Campaigning for banning plastic bags in local businesses
- Regularly hosting a booth in the local community centre to develop awareness about proposed changes to a local law
- Organising a food drive, partnered with a local NGO
- Conducting a waste audit in your school
- Organising a human rights seminar
- Developing and maintaining a website for an NGO abroad

Now brainstorm some other examples of CAS experiences, and clarify what type of service the experience would be.

To what extent do you agree that direct service may offer better opportunities for CAS?

4.03 An explanation of service learning

Since it first emerged with concrete philosophies and guidelines in the 1970s, there have been a number of different ways of understanding service learning. At its very core, service learning is an approach to teaching that combines classroom instruction with students taking action within the community. It provides authentic learning experiences by enabling you to use and develop further the knowledge and skills you have gained from the curriculum in a real setting – to address an identified need and bring about positive community change.

Service learning: is 'a philosophy, pedagogy, and model for community development that is used as an instructional strategy to meet learning goals and/or content standards'.

In a traditional approach to service learning, your subject teacher would play a key role in combining the delivery of the curriculum and participating in activities to address identified community needs. While we encourage you to discuss such opportunities with your subject teachers, an aim of this chapter is for you to explore these opportunities yourself rather than being guided by the perspective of your teachers.

Key point: Service is best conducted when it involves the target community in a number of stages of the experience, from surveying and observation in the Investigation stage, to evaluation in the Reflection stage.

4

Service learning provides you with a unique opportunity to experience your own capacity through the development and application of your knowledge and skills in tasks that others can appreciate. Working with others in community-focused experiences builds relationships and bonds, and frequently contains an emotional element. In this type of experiential learning, not only can you develop problem-solving and collaboration skills, you can also personally contribute to enhancing the lives of others.

Service learning reflects the concept that education implies a social responsibility, and that the most effective learning is actively connected to experience. It is not one-way giving or taking, but rather a social and educational exchange. In this way you and your school are not simply welfare agents; you are taking on real tasks and responsibilities that provide an opportunity for you to further your formal learning.

Your service learning is to be aimed at addressing an identified need, and should be considered as a partnership with the community members you are working with. Consultation, discussion, sharing ideas and collaboration are all elements of this partnership and help to achieve the best benefits for all concerned. Working with others involves meeting new people, gaining new perspectives and developing social awareness while becoming appreciative of the complex nature of the issues faced in our communities – all of these factors can foster your international mindedness.

It is worth further highlighting that of the three characteristics of international mindedness according to the IB – global engagement, multilingualism and intercultural understanding (Singh and Qi, 2013:14) – it is clear that service learning involves at least two of these characteristics, and at times all three!

International mindedness: the knowledge and understanding of self and other cultures that allows for positive interaction; what some may refer to as global citizenship or global competencies.

How internationally minded are you? In what ways do you think that being involved in service learning can contribute to developing your international mindedness?

Supervision of your service learning

While service learning asks that you apply your academic knowledge in real settings, it is not something that you should do without guidance. As you are dealing with real people in real situations, errors may lead to real harm. Supervision by an appropriate adult, sometimes one of your teachers or sometimes a community partner, throughout your application of the CAS stages can help avoid undesired outcomes. It can also ensure that the issues and people you are engaging with will be appropriate for your age, capabilities and maturity levels. After all, we want to ensure that your engagement does not physically or emotionally harm you!

Who might you approach to be a supervisor for a service experience or project? Think wider than just your school community when answering this question.

Your adult supervisor should also support you in critically reflecting on your involvement. As outlined in the previous chapter, reflection is a part of all CAS experiences. However, as service learning often involves interaction with others, dealing first-hand with real issues, this may also expose you to situations that challenge your values, provoke your emotions and confront your perceptions. You would benefit from guided reflection in such situations.

Below are some important points for you to consider when thinking about service learning in your CAS programme.

- Your actions should be in response to an identified community need.
- It is necessary for you to avoid paternalistic assistance, as this does not consider the dignity or rights of others.
- Service projects should be meaningful and involve ongoing reflection.
- Your approach to service learning should be one of social promotion rather than an attitude of assistance.
- You need an adult supervisor to give you guidance and support in your efforts. They are also beneficial in guiding your reflections.
- Your engagement should promote harmony and reciprocity while safeguarding the identity, dignity and initiative of the people involved.
- You must follow the CAS stages in your service learning pursuits.

4.04 The CAS stages and developing service learning

In Chapter 2 we explored the CAS stages, and saw how they act as a framework to use in your CAS experiences. This section will add to those details, giving you additional specific guidance on how to use the CAS stages in service learning. Before we start looking at each stage in detail, let's first look at an example of the stages being applied.

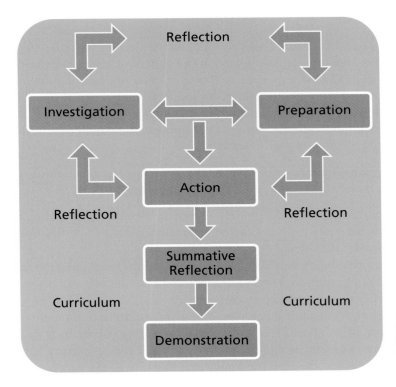

Figure 4.3 CAS stages of service learning.

CAS CASE STUDY

CAS Project: House construction in Cañete

Students from Colegio Alpamayo in Peru joined in a housing construction project with 'Proyecto Hogar' in Lima, Peru.

Investigation

The project first required the students to perform a census in a community near Lima, with the goal of visiting and interviewing families in their own homes. Acknowledging that when conducting interviews they must act with respect for the dignity of the families, the students evaluated the conditions in which families lived, discovering aspects of health and work that helped determine the needs of those families. This information was key in decisions about housing allocation – it also helped serve as a strong motivation for the students to raise economic resources for the houses.

The students also investigated fund-raising, performed market research to assess preferences of the target market and made enquiries into how to achieve good profit margins.

Preparation

The aim of the students was to raise enough money to finance the building of as many houses as possible. As such, the students had to create a number of fund-raising activities that they carried out over a period of eight months, following the development of an overarching fund-raising plan and schedule. Each fund-raising activity required more in-depth planning including costs, roles of team members, and resources required. Preparation related to the house construction took place at a later stage, where students had to develop some basic construction skills and knowledge.

Action

Students implemented their proposals for funds through the following activities:

- Sale of snacks, soda and burgers.

- CAS Cinema. This activity consisted of one group focusing on ticket sales, the other on advertising and food sales. The films were screened in the auditorium of the school with the authorisation of the school's board of directors.

- Collecting money in the Jockey Plaza Mall. In addition to the activities proposed by students and by management of the organisation 'Proyecto Hogar', the students were given permission to perform three collections from the city's busiest mall.

Once the house construction commenced, the students were supported by the organisation of Proyecto Hogar and were committed to building houses for three families. Construction was carried out by 23 students, who overcame obstacles and challenges related to manual labour and developing new skills.

Reflection

With fund-raising activities underway, each group used reflection to learn from and improve their tasks. Reflection was guided and shared among the groups. The learning the students experienced and challenges they faced could be seen in some of the students' reflections:

'During the last two weeks we acted as salesmen in the school. For my part, I did not think I could sell, as I knew that to succeed you have to talk and persuade, and I am not confident in talking upfront. And this being my first time, I did not think that they would buy from me, but they did and I overcame my shyness. I am satisfied with the results, which are actually much better than I expected. I developed some confidence from this.

'From early Saturday morning until late Sunday evening over more than one weekend, we participated in the construction of houses in the community of 'Las Lomas' in San Vicente de Cañete. The houses were pre-fabricated, which meant that there was always a task to be completed and so constant work and creativity are needed – it was a difficult and tiring task! This experience left an imprint on us, as we saw in two days the reality of poverty in which half of Peru's population live. Personally, what prompted me to finish building the houses was observing the situation of the people in the area and still see a smile on their faces. We felt good in helping make a change to the situation of Peruvians living in extreme poverty, and I think this was a very important part of my CAS.'

Mariano

Demonstration

A group of the students involved in the project were invited to join a session in a CAS workshop in Lima, where they shared their experiences, feelings, thoughts, interactions and reflections related to the project. Workshop participants highlighted their participation and testimonies as one of the most significant outcomes of the CAS workshop.

We will now look at using the CAS stages in service learning. You can refer back to Chapter 2 for additional information on implementing the CAS stages.

Investigation

Investigation in service learning is a three-pronged approach – a consideration of your skills and interests, finding a cause that appeals to you, and assessing the community for needs related to your cause and how they can be addressed.

Your skills and interests

In addition to the 'Investigating you' survey in Chapter 2 section 2.01, some additional questions to explore your skills and interests include: What do you enjoy doing in your spare time? What extracurricular activities do you do? Which are your best subjects? What skills would your friends say you had? What skills would your teachers say you had?

Responding to questions such as these, which in itself is a reflection exercise, is aimed at providing you with some direction for how you might engage in a service learning project or what possible roles and responsibilities might suit you. For example, a student who enjoys writing and is a member of a journalism club could take on the role of media and marketing manager, or a student who loves sport may wish to explore possibilities for service in the community involving sports.

Finding a cause

In this investigation you want to find out more about what possible issues you want to address. As shown in Chapter 2 section 2.01, there are a number of global issues that you could engage with. This section involves identifying those that you really want to do something about.

> **Key point:** When you are in the process of finding a cause and identifying that it is a need to be addressed in a community, you are uncovering an opportunity to make a change.

If you are still having difficulties in finding a cause after completing the exercise shown in Chapter 2 section 2.01, then the activity below may assist you in identifying an issue or a cause to support.

4

Start by thinking about the 'pros' and 'cons' of your community – what are some of the positive things about it? What are some of the things that cause you concern or need to change?

Next, consider what your ideal community would look like. What would it be like if the 'cons' you listed above did not exist?

Now, think about what kinds of things could be done to create your ideal community. What role could you play in taking these actions? Do not ignore the challenges faced in creating your ideal community – these things do not just happen overnight. You also need to consider these barriers as you establish some concrete actions that you could take.

You now have a list of actions that could be taken to improve your community, and which show how you could possibly be involved in them. The next step would be to investigate these further to see what other members of the community think, and to validate them as identified needs. The investigation phase could also involve discussing these ideas with some of your friends, not only to hear their perspective, but to also see if they would be interested in partnering with you.

Identifying a community need

While it is important that you get involved in a cause that you are interested in, the success of your project also hinges on how relevant your cause is – there is no point in trying to fix something if it does not need to be fixed!

Some questions you can consider here include: Why does this issue need to be addressed? What would happen if nothing was done about it? Why do people in the community care about this? The important point here is that you cannot answer these questions yourself – you must do some research so that people who have a good understanding about these issues, and the members of the community where you think the need is, can contribute to the responses to these questions.

Key point: Service learning involves engaging yourself in addressing an identified need. You must therefore verify this need in the Investigation stage.

Some ways of finding out more

Ask ...

Develop a set of questions for a survey that will allow you to obtain a lot of information about what people feel and think about certain issues in their community. Be very careful in developing your questions so that you avoid any bias or leading questions – it would be best to ask a teacher to check your questions before you send them out. Consider online survey tools to make your data collection more efficient.

Meet ...

Seeking information from primary sources is very important. Having conversations with community members or people knowledgeable about your chosen issue to find out their viewpoint is a good way of seeking first-hand information. Again, it is important that you develop appropriate questions that are first checked by your teacher.

Look ...

Take the time to observe the community, focusing on people's actions and behaviours and how the issues you are considering manifest themselves. Take note of key points that you observe, as well as any thoughts that your observations may provoke.

Read ...

The media can be a valuable source of information about communities and the issues they face. Read local newspapers or any online material such as blogs, focusing on both the community you are aiming to work with and the issues you are thinking about addressing. Videos or other online clips may also be useful. There may be existing data on the issue or the community you are focusing on. Research to see if studies related to your need or community have already been conducted, or statistics collected by government agencies or other organisations. Do make sure though that you consider the reliability, currency and validity of your sources.

Now we will look at some questions that you may wish to ask a potential community partner as a part of your investigation.

4

The following survey questions could be used during the Investigation stage to gather information about an NGO that you may wish to use as a partner in your CAS efforts. Gathering detailed information about a potential community partner is essential to establish whether their goals and philosophy align with your own.

- What are the goals of your organisation?
- How and when did your organisation begin?
- What issues do your organisation work in addressing?
- What have been some successes?
- What have been some of the barriers you have had to face in doing your work?
- How many people are involved with your organisation?
- What role do volunteers play in your organisation? What do people need to do to volunteer for your organisation?
- How is your organisation funded? What policies do you have about your expenditure? How do you provide accountability to your benefactors?

SPOTLIGHT ON ... INVESTIGATION

ConCERT – 'Connecting Communities, Environment and Responsible Tourism' – is a not-for-profit social enterprise based in Siem Reap, Cambodia, whose vision is a Cambodia free of poverty. Michael Horton, chairman and founder, established ConCERT in 2008 to guide and advise the increasing numbers of people who wish to offer their help while visiting Cambodia, thus turning good intentions into the best possible help for the most vulnerable people. Their slogan is 'Helping you to Help' and neatly sums up the group's aims. Here Michael responds to questions relevant to working with other communities as a part of a CAS, and especially to volunteering abroad.

If students were interested in supporting members of a community abroad, what is some advice you would give them?
Do some research about the community you will visit before you travel. Make direct contact with the organisation or community project you aim to be involved with in plenty of time, and find out what you will be doing. Those you contact should be willing to give you plenty of information about their work, their needs, what you will be doing and

how you will be supported. Also let them know what your goals are for your trip, especially those that relate to your volunteer placement with them. Also, find out if they have any priority needs for resources that you may be able to bring from home.

What makes a successful volunteer placement, and what can go wrong if these requirements are not in place?
Volunteering can bring benefits for all concerned. The best placements enable the volunteer to have a rewarding experience while also bringing useful support to the project and the people it serves. Firstly, you need to ask some questions. When you volunteer, especially in a foreign country, you rely heavily on the guidance and support of those in charge. You quite reasonably assume many things about the project where you'll be working, and you need to be sure that these basic requirements are in place:

1 Does the project where you'll be working meet a real need, and is it the appropriate response to that need? (There is, for example, much concern from projects such as UNICEF, Save The Children, Friends International and others, that, in many instances, orphanages are not the right response to the needs of poor Cambodian children.)

2 Is the programme run by people who have extensive knowledge of the issues that their project is trying to address?

3 Does the project operate on sound principles? Is it well managed and financially transparent?

4 Is your volunteer input really needed, and will it contribute to improving the situation?

5 If your work is with vulnerable people (such as children, young adults, people with learning or other disabilities, or people in extreme poverty), are there appropriate measures in place to protect these people and yourself?

6 Will you have adequate supervision and guidance, and will your tasks be clearly explained?

7 If required, will you have general support to cope with life in a country where so many things are different? Have reasonable steps been taken to ensure your safety?

By contrast, inappropriate volunteering can undermine local people's confidence, impose the volunteer's agenda, increase the dependency on outside help, unwittingly support and perpetuate questionable projects and practices, take away jobs from local people, and create more problems than it solves.

What are some of the steps ConCERT takes in assessing community needs?

The first and most important thing that ConCERT wants to know is, 'Does the project truly understand the problems it is trying to address?' We then want to know if its programmes are effective in helping these problems. We also want to know whether the project is clear about who the beneficiaries are, how it is managed, and why and how it uses and supports volunteers.

When considering supporting a particular NGO, what are some of the things that students should consider before working with the organisation?

1 Ask what has been achieved by previous volunteers.

2 Be clear about how your money is being used. Will the money you raise go to a project, or is some kept for overheads and over expenses? Ensure that the organisation is transparent about their expenditure.

3 Be wary if the organisation:
   • resists putting you in touch with previous volunteers or local people if you ask
   • doesn't clearly explain where and how you fit into their overall plans
   • doesn't ask many questions about you (except how you are going to pay).

Figure 4.4 ConCERT – helping volunteers in their investigation and preparation for service.

In what ways may some of these points apply for a service experience conducted locally? How might you incorporate some of these thoughts about investigation to your service?

CAS CASE STUDY

Open Mike – An example of Investigation in a CAS service learning experience

Investigation: Following class content on the composition of songs, a group of music students decided that they would like to have an 'open mike concert' in the school. They brainstormed some ideas and discussed these with their music teacher. They conducted an informal survey to gather some feedback from the student body, and refined some of their ideas around logistics.

As they collected information, their ideas developed into having the open mike event open to all levels at the school, aiming to provide an opportunity for singer-songwriters in the school to share their talents. Guidelines were created around what entries needed to involve. They set a date which was very much dependent upon the school calendar and available dates for the school's performing arts theatre. Further investigation went into what resources might be required, and how they could best promote their event, which included research on social media and marketing. During their investigation the students decided to use the open mike event as an awareness and fund-raising event for an NGO that one of the students had a previous connection with. Members of the group met with a representative of the NGO, and brainstormed some ideas of how to support the NGO in reaching their goals.

Preparation

Once you have a clear idea on what community need you wish to address, and you have developed your SMART goals (see Chapter 2 section 2.01), you can get involved in preparing to take action. Keep in mind that as you develop your action plan – indicating what tasks need to be completed, who is going to complete them and by when, as well as what resources might be required – you may need to go back to the Investigation stage to seek more information.

Key point: The boundaries between the Investigation and Preparation stages are not clear-cut; there is often some going back and forth between these stages as you plan your service learning engagement.

4

Not only is it wise to consult community partners when developing your plans, it may even be best to collaborate with them. It is also essential that you seek feedback on your action plan before you commence its implementation. Your adult supervisor, as well as others who have knowledge in the areas of your project goals or the issue you are addressing, should give you guidance and feedback on your plans. Your teacher of a subject that has clear connections to your service learning project will be a very valuable resource here, not only in providing advice on your ideas and plans, but also in developing the subject knowledge and skills that you have identified as essential to be able to proceed with your plans, and with implementing them.

There are certain actions or tasks that are found in many service learning projects, some of which take place in the Preparation stage. These include, but are not limited to, writing proposals (and often presenting them), seeking sponsorship or other types of funding, developing a budget, and promotion and marketing, including making use of the media. Let's look at each of these in more detail.

Developing a proposal

The content of your proposal depends upon its purpose – you may be submitting your proposal to seek approval from your CAS Coordinator or your school, or you may be submitting it to potential donors or community partners. You need to consider the target audience and exactly what information they need. The following outlines some generic sections to include in your proposal:

- service learning project information
- title of service learning project
- names of students involved
- project team leader/s
- adult supervisor
- project mission statement (What is the purpose of the project?/What do you hope to achieve?)
- project summary – including project rationale, specific goals, budget statement and an overview of your plan
- time frame (commencing and completion dates).

Creating a budget

If your service learning involves any costs, then you need to calculate how much and consider where you will source funds for your expenditure. Developing your budget is best done in a spreadsheet that will make it easier to produce your calculations. It should include the items or resources you need, the amount you need and their total cost. Consider also where you could source funds to cover the costs. Here you should also consider 'in-kind' donations, which is when a donor supplies the actual goods you need, rather than money to cover their costs.

Item/resource	Number required	Total cost	Possible funding source

Table 4.1 An example budget template.

Seeking sponsorship

A sponsorship proposal is used to seek funds, or in-kind donations required for your project. In some ways, a sponsorship proposal is similar to a project proposal, with information about your aims, rationale, and what action you will be taking. What is also needed in a sponsorship proposal is the amount of cash or kind that you are requesting, and the benefits that the sponsor (donor) would receive in return. Possible benefits include giving the donor publicity, product promotions, advertising and general exposure to the public.

Key point: We cannot always rely on the goodwill of people to donate money or goods. As such, we can use some incentive to persuade them to give, something that shows how they would benefit from their support. If a potential donor is a business, having that business understand how supporting your event could benefit their business interests would increase the likelihood of them providing the support you need.

Promotion and marketing

Letting others know about your service learning project is important to gain support for your efforts and help achieve your goals. Promoting your project can assist you in seeking volunteers to join your cause, may assist in seeking donors, can help with networking and connecting with others who are involved in a similar cause, and, importantly, can help increase public awareness about the community need you are addressing.

4

In all forms of marketing, you need to consider: your target audience; the message you wish to give; the most efficient, and in some cases cost-effective, way of reaching your audience. Some forms of promotion and marketing include:

- social media
- flyers/leaflets
- posters/banners
- website/blogs
- newsletters
- blogs
- email marketing
- face-to-face promotions in public places/events
- magazine or newspaper articles (refer to the following section below, 'The media')
- word of mouth.

The media

The media can be a useful tool to help promote and market your service learning experience. You may use the media at certain phases of your project – before, during or after. In all cases, you would create a press release and send this to targeted newspapers, online publications or magazines in the hope that they would publish your article. As with promoting your event, you need to consider your target audience and the message you wish to give. A press release will commonly follow the '5 Ws' format:

- Who is/was involved in the project?
- What happened, or what are you planning to happen?
- Where did it/will it take place?
- When did it/will it occur?
- Why did it/will it happen? (What are the goals of your project?)

Press release: also referred to as a media release, this is a written statement or article provided to media outlets announcing certain details of a newsworthy event.

Continuing with our 'Open Mike' CAS Snapshot, let's look at some of the points completed by these students during the Preparation stage.

CAS SNAPSHOT

Open Mike – An example of Preparation in a CAS service learning experience

Some tasks that the students listed in their action plan included promotion and marketing, logistics and bookings, auditions, stage management and event running sheet, budget, rules and judging, fund-raising and NGO-awareness. Some of the equipment the group needed to provide included microphones, amplifiers, mixing boards, musical instruments, lighting and cables. Promotional material, both for the event and on the NGO, needed to be developed. A technical team had to be assembled for the night and 'front of house' team to help control audiences and collect funds for the charity assembled. A representative of the charity was contacted and invited to attend the night, giving a short speech during the evening and also presenting the winner with their prize.

Action

You are what you do, not what you say you'll do.

C. G. Jung

This stage involves turning your ideas into action. Service learning involves much planning – before you act you need to have clear, well-detailed plans based on much investigation. Your action plan will detail what type of service you will use – direct service, indirect service, advocacy or research. Remember to collect documentation of your engagement that you can later use in the Demonstration stage!

Something you must avoid is taking action with little or no planning, or taking action with no clearly defined goals. This is sometimes the case when students consider service and how they can benefit somebody. Rather than investigate the complex issues they could engage with, they simply come to the conclusion that they could support somebody or address an issue simply by conducting some fund-raising. 'Can we hold a bake sale?' is a question that is too often asked of CAS Coordinators without much investigation or preparation. Though fund-raising can certainly be a positive part of your CAS portfolio, it should not be your first thought; it must come after much research and consideration of the various ways you can take action. And if your investigation does indicate that fund-raising can be a part of your service action, do consider the numerous ways you can generate funds. You would benefit from the creativity and challenge that is involved in developing and implementing fund-raising plans rather than choosing the easy option of holding a bake sale.

SPOTLIGHT ON ... FUND-RAISING

While fund-raising can be a valuable experience, may benefit the recipient of the funds raised, and be a worthwhile learning opportunity for those students involved, this is only the case if fund-raising is 'done well'. The danger with fund-raising is that it sometimes exists for its own sake, with those students involved as organisers or as participants not gaining any understanding of the issues that the funds are being raised for. Fund-raising can also create an oversimplified point of view on how to solve global issues: raising money for a cause does not necessarily mean that underlying issues are addressed or that problems are solved.

Fund-raising should always provide an opportunity for learning – for those involved in organising fund-raising activities and those who are participating. Learning should be based on the underlying issues, about other ways that people can get involved in making a difference and, if applicable, about the organisation being supported and their goals. UK-based organisation 'Think Global' has worked with a number of NGOs to produce a guide for students involved in fund-raising (refer to the reference list at the end of this chapter for more details on the guide). Some key points that it suggests include:

- learn more about the underlying issues that funds are being raised to address

- explore the work of charities and NGOs

- consider other actions that can be taken to effect change.

Something to also consider when looking at getting involved in fund-raising is to ask – is there something else I can do? Might there be other action I can take?

Let's now return to our 'Open Mike' CAS Snapshot to see what these students were involved in during the Action stage.

CAS CASE STUDY

Open Mike – An example of Action in a CAS service learning experience

The night of the open mike event proved to be a great success, with the singer-songwriters a small part of a large and at times chaotic programme. This indirect service experience involved a number of students performing various tasks, coordinated by two group leaders. The organisers had a few teething problems in double-booking equipment, and some communication issues, but the performers took this in their stride and let their talent shine through. The NGO that was being supported was glad for the exposure they received and the money that was raised.

Figure 4.5 Open Mike – a service learning opportunity for Diploma music students.

4 Reflection

The nature of service learning – its involvement of working with others, who in many cases are from a different culture and situation from yours, seeing first-hand the impact that issues have on communities, examining these complex issues, hearing different perspectives and developing relationships with the people you work with – encourages a greater frequency of reflection. Reflection here plays a key role in making sense of the impact that your CAS involvement is having on you and on others, in considering your thoughts and feelings, and in exploring how you may apply your learning in different contexts. The transformational power of service is best supported through regular, ongoing reflection.

In addition to details outlined in Chapter 2 section 2.04 and in Chapter 3, some specific questions to consider in the Reflection stage of service learning include:

• What impact has your involvement had on you? And on others?
• What does your involvement mean to you? And to others in the community?
• How have your skills and knowledge in your subject area/s developed?
• In which ways has your involvement challenged you?
• What personal attributes have been exposed from your involvement?
• What different ways of thinking or acting have you been exposed to?
• What have you learnt about the community you are working with?

CAS CASE STUDY

Open Mike – An example of Reflection in a CAS service learning experience

In addition to individual reflections that students added to their personal CAS portfolios, the students involved in the Open Mike concert had a final reflective session with the music teacher and the staff member that supported them in their efforts. The students reflected positively on the experience and said that they had learnt a lot about organising an event. The biggest issue that they had faced was the level of communication that they needed with all of the groups, and students reflected that it was so important to have face-to-face communication with people as sometimes people did not read or respond to emails or text messages. An additional challenge was coordinating the various venues and equipment that they needed at each venue.

Demonstration

As explained in Chapter 2, demonstration involves displaying your CAS efforts. In a service learning project, this often involves more than sharing your efforts in your CAS portfolio, as you may have a responsibility to report to certain stakeholders involved in the project. Demonstrating your service may also act to increase awareness about the issue or community need you were addressing, or both! As it could also act to inspire others to get involved in service, your CAS Coordinator may request that you showcase your efforts at a particular school event.

Bear in mind the following when considering how to demonstrate your service learning:

- Create a report to provide to funders or sponsors, the school board or other stakeholders connected to the engagement. This could be written, visual or verbal.
- Make use of the media – develop a press release aiming to inform the public about your project.
- Make use of online media to celebrate your project.
- Host a culminating event, inviting the public as well as stakeholders to join you in showcasing your CAS. Create displays and deliver speeches.
- If applicable, share your accomplishments, and thank volunteers and participants.

CAS CASE STUDY

Open Mike – An example of Demonstration in a CAS service learning experience

An article on Open Mike was written by the students and included in the school newsletter. This article was also sent to the local newspaper, which included it along with a photograph of the event. A member of the organising group was invited to speak about their event to younger students at the school at a year-level assembly.

4

4.05 Exploring service learning opportunities in the Diploma Programme curriculum

Including service learning in the *CAS Guide* aims to direct you to a planned and thoughtful approach to your service experiences. It also allows for an authentic connection between CAS and other Diploma Programme subject areas. Now let's take a look at some examples where students have connected their CAS service experiences to their subject curriculum.

Geography

A topic within the IB core topic of Populations in Transitions is about migration and the issues that migrants face when they arrive in another country. Inspired by this topic, a group of students discovered the opportunity to work with young migrants in the Swiss city of Zurich. They assisted these migrants with different issues they had in using the German language. This also helped the students to reinforce their own German language skills that they were using for the course in German B. As these migrants tended to live together in the same area of the city, the students also started to understand the idea of diaspora, a topic they covered in the curriculum.

Theatre

After connections were made with an NGO supporting migrant workers by the CAS Coordinator and the theatre teacher, students created theatre workshops for migrants. Migrants came to the school weekly to participate in workshops developed by the students. This then evolved into the students working with the migrants to create a production aiming to spread awareness about the plight of the migrant workers. Migrant workers became the cast and also contributed to the script, while students coordinated the set design, lighting and sound, as well as directing the production. The funds raised from ticket sales from the two public shows were donated to the NGO.

Sports, exercise and health science

A sports, exercise and health science student took the role of a personal trainer as a part of his CAS. He advertised his services to the staff of the school, seeking those who wished to improve their health and fitness. Two support staff and a teacher took up the challenge. The student administered fitness tests and then developed specific fitness training programmes based on the results and the desired outcomes of the participants. The programmes were 12 weeks in length, and involved the student regularly observing training sessions and monitoring progress of the participants. Also demonstrating Creativity, the student needed to develop knowledge beyond the curriculum on energy systems, exercise physiology and measurement, and evaluation of human performance.

Biology

Students who were studying HL Biology were interested in extending their studies of a local wetland. Following data collection completed as a part of their course, the students continued with their research by conducting more observations on the wetland ecosystem, conducting a population study of frog species. The students contributed their research to a study being conducted by their local university on that particular ecosystem. The students worked with researchers from the university to ensure that they used proper data collection methods. They were very excited that their work would be used in the study.

History

A Jewish student connected strongly with a part of the IB Diploma History, namely Paper 2, World History Topic 11: Causes and effects of 20th-century wars. The student's class was focusing on the Final Solution as a part of studying the impact of war on domestic populations. This sparked an interest and a desire to take action in the student, who was already concerned about the current spread of racism and in particular the attacks on Jewish groups in France and elsewhere. He decided to explore this further and contact the local Jewish organisation as a part of his investigation into what action he could take. The student discovered that there was a survivor from Auschwitz, one of the extermination camps, still alive and living not too far from the school. With some planning and discussion with his History teacher, and seeking permission from his secondary Principal after submitting a proposal, the student made contact with the person concerned and invited him to come and speak at the school to raise awareness of the Final Solution. The student first met the survivor and discussed the content of his presentation. The survivor then came to the school and spoke of the change in his host nation, and how the police cooperated with the Gestapo to condemn him and his fellow Jews to be transported to Auschwitz. The survivor talked about what happened at Auschwitz and the arbitrary decision about who survived or died. The presentation was immediately followed by a question session and debrief that the student led, with support from his History teacher.

Business and Management

Inspired by content from their Business and Management course, a small group of students initiated a CAS project that involved selling water bottles to raise awareness and funds for a local NGO. The group investigated their possible markets and came up with a product that they thought would help them achieve their goal of raising funds and awareness. The students undertook some market research, conducted a breakdown analysis and pricing plan, created a branding and marketing plan as well as developed ideas for product placement. The group's teacher took the opportunity to hold some additional lunchtime lessons with the group, revising curriculum content that related and supported the group's CAS project.

Environmental Systems and Societies (ESS)

Two students, whose concerns about the natural environment increased due to their involvement in their ESS course, conducted research involving transect sampling to write a report on a mangrove ecosystem located close to the school. The students, who had already conducted similar data collection as a part of their course, collected data on landscape succession and monitored flora and fauna. They used this data to write a research report that they presented to the school council and a local councillor as part of a proposal for the school to initiate a mangrove conservation project.

Economics

A group of Economics students in Thailand researched self-help groups within the area of development economics. Building on what the students learnt in the classroom, they conducted some online research looking at methods of microfinance in self-help groups in various contexts in India and Thailand. With guidance from their Economics teacher, the students further investigated initiating a self-help group in a community near their school, made contact with groups in India involved in supporting self-help groups for ideas and guidance, and worked with leaders in their local community to help set up a group. Months of work led to a microfinance system implemented using a self-help group in the community, with students guiding community leaders in planning and implementation.

These scenarios provide some concrete examples of service learning in CAS, and demonstrate how you can benefit from a theoretical approach to service: making use of, and further developing, academic skills and knowledge through the application of the CAS stages for service learning. Not only can this increase your subject knowledge and understanding, making learning real by applying it in real-life settings, but it can also increase the likelihood of your service goals being attained.

4

4.06 Review of Chapter 1

1   What does service learning mean to you?

2   How might service learning complement your understanding in your Diploma Programme subjects?

3   Concentrating on the subjects you take in your Diploma Programme, what specific skills or knowledge from your subjects could you utilise in a service learning project?

4   What role do you think your subject teachers could take in your CAS programme? How could they be used as a resource?

4.07 A summary of this chapter

In this chapter we have:

*   Considered the different types of service that you could engage in within your CAS programme
*   Outlined best practice to approaching service in CAS
*   Explained the concept of service learning and explored how it can be approached in CAS
*   Examined the CAS stages for service learning and looked at examples of its use
*   Provided examples of service learning opportunities.

CAS, TOK and the extended essay

5

The core of the Diploma Programme – CAS, TOK and the extended essay – is a key part of what makes this curriculum unique. Its holistic approach, which aims to develop you as an individual and not just concentrate on your academic capabilities, its attention to developing international mindedness, its focus on developing your critical thinking and reflective skills, and the way it encourages you to make combined use of the skills and knowledge you gain in your subject areas, justifies these three areas being central to the Diploma Programme. This is where the IB learner profile really comes to life!

This chapter will explore the relationship between CAS and the other elements of Diploma Programme core. We will start with a look at the coherence of the core – the three aims that each of the elements of the core contribute to – then focus on the specific relationships between CAS and TOK, and between CAS and the extended essay. We will offer a number of activities to help you make meaningful connections between these areas, which will benefit not only your CAS efforts but also your understanding and progress in TOK and the extended essay. A number of practical examples of CAS experiences that link with other core elements will be explained.

5.01 CAS, the extended essay and TOK

All three elements of the core of the IB Diploma are trying to achieve the same goals. They want to help you, the student to become: internationally minded, clearer about your own values, and aware of the holistic nature of the Diploma. Let's explore these concepts further.

Becoming internationally minded

This means being able to understand and appreciate other cultures through your own experiences and developing a deeper appreciation of another culture through the use of its language. Additionally, the three core elements are there to help you appreciate the values of other cultures that you come into contact with. We live in a time where every place in the world has a migrant community living in it, which means that we are constantly in touch with other cultures. The process of globalisation continues to take effect in every corner of our planet, so it is very important to develop a sense of international mindedness (which involves looking at knowledge on a global scale and using the languages we know). Knowledge taught in schools is usually very Eurocentric, and it is important to realise that other cultures have built knowledge in their own ways, which is just as valuable as Eurocentric knowledge. Ask fellow students to name some scientists: most of the time, they will mention European, male scientists. Information about scientists can be found easily nowadays, and the question that TOK would encourage us to ask is, 'Why do we have such a narrow view of scientific work?'

Becoming clearer about your own values

A key element of the TOK course is for you to think constantly about the knowledge you have and how you acquired it, and to ask questions about your values and perspectives and what may have shaped them. TOK forces us to analyse our feelings and thoughts, and to look at the moral and ethical values that we hold through the lens of ethical systems. In the extended essay students are required to adopt a clear and strict code of academic honesty and ethical approach to research, just as they are in other areas of the Diploma Programme. This requires the researcher to think very carefully about the processes involved in finding and making use of information in a proper manner. One also acquires responsibility through the new ideas that are developed through research. Some other questions can be posed:

- Am I a better person because I do something for others?
- To what extent can CAS make us more aware of our social responsibilities?
- To what extent can a student decide how and who to help in a community?
- What do we mean by 'help' or 'work together', or 'poor' or 'needy'?
- What kinds of values are expressed in our definitions?
- Does a community 'owe' something to IB students?

Key point: The three elements of the core work together to educate the whole person.

5

Becoming aware of the holistic nature of the Diploma

All three elements of the core can be linked to academic subjects, and can support and be supported by them. CAS can be linked to the academic subjects by the practice of service learning (outlined in Chapter 4) where there is a conscious link between the academic subjects and service activities. The TOK links to the subjects through the areas of knowledge (AOK) and the knowledge frameworks. These examine the scope, language, methodology and history of each of the subjects. TOK issues arise in all of your classes.

However, the key feature that links the three core elements is that they all rely on reflection for learning. In this chapter we shall explore how reflection in TOK and the extended essay can influence and effect reflection in CAS. However, we also need to be clear about the differences in reflection between the three elements.

ACTIVITY BOX

Can you complete these statements about reflection in the core?

Reflection in CAS focuses on …

Reflection in TOK focuses on …

Reflection in the extended essay focuses on …

5.02 CAS and TOK

The TOK course is focused on how we absorb knowledge. There is a diagram in the *TOK Guide* that suggests we receive knowledge from two sources: see Figure 5.1.

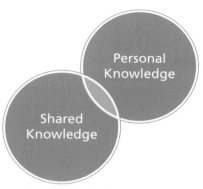

Figure 5.1   The sources of knowledge in the TOK.

CAS experiences help us to gain knowledge. We acquire personal knowledge from new experiences by learning about our skills and ourselves. Shared knowledge comes from the people and groups in the community that we work with. Knowledge is, by its own nature, a social enterprise. We build our own humanity based on sharing knowledge. Basic and essential things such as language only occur if we are with others. For example, interaction with homeless or disabled people offers the opportunity to gain both kinds of knowledge. This can be complementary of other knowledge acquired in a different way, for example, if we are touched by a work of art that show some of those experiences such as a novel, poem or photograph.

ACTIVITY BOX

1   What do you think is our most reliable source of knowledge?

2   Why do you think this?

3   What personal knowledge could you gain from CAS experiences? (give two examples)

4   And how is this knowledge different from the one you gained from previous experiences?

5   What knowledge could you gain from working with others doing CAS experiences? (give two examples)

6   What knowledge do you think could be gained by others from you?

7   How reliable do you think this knowledge would be?

5

Knowledge claims and questions

In this section we are looking at how we can apply the knowledge we gain from CAS to TOK. An important part of the IB Diploma is seeing how one part of the core can support another. You could discuss some of these issues in your TOK class.

A knowledge claim in TOK is really a statement about knowledge that we have gained. For example:

'Our emotions about a group have a large effect on our ability to learn from the group.'

This is a statement about how we are going to acquire knowledge. You will notice that it does not mention a specific situation. In TOK we then ask a 'knowledge question' based on the methods that we have used to acquire knowledge. We are interested to see if the methods are appropriate and produce valid and reliable answers.

Knowledge question: a carefully devised question that leads to inquiry about claims about knowledge, and about knowledge itself. It is a core learning tool in TOK.

Knowledge questions:

a are open-ended (this means that there is no right or wrong answer; in fact there can be many appropriate answers)

b are general questions and not subject- or context-specific

c commonly begin with: to what extent, how far, how, what role, under what circumstances?

The example below shows how an experience in CAS could lead you to develop a claim about knowledge and then ask a knowledge question.

CAS SNAPSHOT

A student works in a soup kitchen and has the chance to both meet the organisers and also many of the clients. Two of the supervisors make some generalisations that the people that come to visit the soup kitchen are in poor health and many of them have had problems with either alcohol or drug addiction. As a consequence they have experienced break-ups with their wives or partners, and many of them are very unhappy. The student's personal perception of the clients at the soup kitchen is that they are in poor health as they have skin blemishes, are extremely thin and often have poor personal hygiene.

Based on the knowledge that has been gained from this CAS experience, we could make the following knowledge claim and knowledge question:

Knowledge claim: We can rely on our sense perceptions to judge a person's health.

Knowledge question: To what extent can we rely on our perception to tell us the truth?

Figure 5.2 Helping to serve food in a soup kitchen.

Let's develop a knowledge question from a CAS experience you have been involved in, by first thinking about the knowledge you have gained, and then making a claim about this knowledge.

5

- Can you think of a CAS experience where you have gained some knowledge?
- Using this CAS experience, make a claim about knowledge.
- Then see if you can frame a knowledge question based on the knowledge claim you have made (this could help you in preparing a TOK presentation or essay, which is covered later in the chapter).

The ways of knowing and reflection in CAS

As we saw in Chapter 3, an important part of the TOK course is the ways of knowing (WOKs). There are eight WOKs that have been identified in the TOK course as helping us to understand how we gain knowledge. The following WOKs are mentioned in TOK: language, memory, emotion, sense–perception, imagination, intuition, faith and reason. Each of these WOKs has some influence on how you gain information from your CAS experiences and also how you reflect on them.

Way of knowing	Questions that we might ask to help reflections in CAS
Language	1. When our experience involves interacting with people from another culture, how much meaning do we lose in translation? 2. To what extent do stereotypes affect how we behave in a CAS experience?
Memory	1. To what extent does memory affect our recollection of a CAS experience? 2. To what extent do special cues to help us remember? 3. What is the role of History, Maths or Sciences in social work?
Emotion	1. How does our body language affect our relationships with others? 2. What level of objectivity do we have about our relationships with others? 3. What is the role of curiosity and empathy in a CAS project?
Sense-perception	1. To what degree can we trust our senses to give us a picture of an experience? 2. Does one sense affect our CAS experience over the others? 3. How do our values and social context influence what we perceive or expect in a given situation?
Imagination	1. To what extent can we gain knowledge from experiences without imagination? 2. How much is it possible to learn a new skill without the use of imagination? 3. What is the role of imagination (and intuition) in making decisions on emerging problems or understanding new cultural contexts?

Intuition	1. To what extent do we rely on a connection between intuition and instincts to make decisions? 2. To what extent do we rely on inference to gain knowledge from CAS experiences?
Faith	1. To what extent can we rely on the judgement of others in gaining knowledge from them? 2. Is experience the most reliable source of information?
Reason	1. How much do we rely on deduction to gain knowledge? 2. To what extent is what we might consider 'reasonable' accurate in other contexts?

CAS SNAPSHOT

'On our second day in the "Peterhof" we started spending time with disabled people. We drew pictures and brushed the teeth of the patients. I found it difficult to let the patients touch me at the beginning. They just came to you and wanted to hold your hand and hug you. I got acquainted with D—, a very sweet girl in her 20s. She was very nice and we became friends from the first minute! I believe she showed me her affection by kissing my hand on first seeing me. I also got to know 26-year old O—, a girl in a wheelchair, who suffered from spasticity. I fed her, but it was very difficult, as she couldn't swallow the mash in the right way.

'I also went with another volunteer and two disabled women to the playground. They both were extremely happy that they could go outside and enjoy the fresh air. During the time we were there, there was a quarantine where all of the disabled people were sick and not allowed to go outside. So when we bought a Coke for these two ladies, they screamed with happiness. I was so happy to experience this moment of joy.'

Taken from reflections of students at Salem College in Germany.

One important WOK, equally exercised by scientists, intellectuals, artists and students, is that of curiosity – a powerful emotion that compels us to search for knowledge. Before you choose your EE topic or CAS project you must have a strong sense of curiosity. Let's now consider the WOKs in your CAS.

5

CAS and the AOK

Can you name the eight AOK that there are for TOK? Each AOK has a knowledge framework: see Table 5.1

AOK	Knowledge framework
Scope/applications	This looks at the range of topics within the subject area and which are current concerns.
Language and concepts	This is the vocabulary that is unique to the subject area and distinguishes it from other AOKs. There are concepts, models and axioms that are also specific to the subject area (e.g. Newton's laws of gravity are specific to the Natural Sciences).
Methodology	The methods used to obtain knowledge that are specific to that subject. An example would be the scientific method where a claim is made about knowledge and then tested to see if that claim is false or not.
Historical development of the subject	The focal point here is the shifts in thinking that have occurred over time. What are the current interests of the subject? Which problems is the subject trying to solve?
Personal knowledge	The knowledge that an individual has of a particular subject.

Table 5.1   AOK in the knowledge framework

CAS and ethics

One of the AOKs that has an effect on the way that we gain knowledge from CAS is ethics. It is important to remember that ethics works in tandem with WOKs, especially reason and emotions.

Let's start our focus on CAS and ethics by looking at a student reflection. Consider here the ethical decision that the student is reflecting on, as well as the role that reason and emotion may have played in this decision. The reflection is on a dance project that involved this student co-producing dance performance.

CAS SNAPSHOT

'Nicole came to rehearsal one day on crutches with a leg in a soft cast. It turns out that she had torn a muscle, and was unable to dance for two to four weeks. This was a big concern for us, because the show was seven weeks' away, and the next few weeks were crucial for learning the dance steps. Choreographers couldn't afford to spend any extra time teaching her the dance moves when she was able to dance again, and even by the time she would be able to dance, she might not necessarily have been able to completely exert herself.

'Katrina and I unfortunately had to make the decision to exclude her from the show – I understood how devastated she was not to be able to perform, but it was just as hard for us to let her go. I've learnt here that it's important for me to be professional and practical, no matter what I feel.'

Phoebe, United World College of South East Asia, Singapore.

Ethics: also referred to as moral philosophy, 'involves systematising, defending, and recommending concepts of right and wrong behaviour'. Fieser, n.d.

The above CAS Snapshot provides us with just one example of an ethical decision that came about through CAS. The CAS Teacher Support Material makes this important point about such ethical decisions in CAS:

5

Human actions are never neutral; they
always have consequences for one's self, for
others, for the community. The outcomes
may enhance or diminish well-being, acting
towards the welfare of all the people involved
or decreasing the quality of our lives or their
lives. Making ethically valid decisions requires
skilled ethical reasoning, based on ethical
concepts and principles.

CAS Teacher Support Material (2015), page 50, IBO

In TOK we look at the different types of ethical systems, listed here.

Ethical relativism

No principles are universally valid. All moral principles are valid relative
to cultural tastes. The rules of society serve as a standard.

Divine command theory

Moral standards depend on a God that is all-knowing. Any act that
conforms to the laws of God is right, an act that in a way that breaks the
laws of God is wrong.

Utilitarianism

Actions are judged right or wrong solely by their consequences. Right
actions are those that produce the greatest balance of happiness over
unhappiness. Each person's happiness is equally important.

Deontology

The emphasis here is on a set of moral rules and duty. Human beings
are given a special status and all people enjoy the same rights. People are
treated as ends, not means.

Virtue ethics

Morals are internal. Virtue ethics seek to produce good people who
act well out of spontaneous goodness. This system of ethics emphasises
living well and achieving excellence.

Which of these ethical systems has influenced some of your actions in a CAS experience? Give an example of one of them.

In CAS we are also concerned with acting in an ethical way. The seventh learning outcomes is 'Recognize and consider the ethics of choices and actions'.

CAS Guide (2015), page 50, IBO

ACTIVITY BOX

1 Give examples of ethical decisions you have made in the following contexts:
   a in sport
   b in carrying out a service experience
   c in dealing with other people
   d in terms of academic honesty
   e reflection.

2 Which ethical system most influenced your decisions?

3 How often do we make decisions in CAS relative to the feelings of our peer group?

Developing an ethical identity requires you to develop ethical capacities as a complete person, using your ability to think, feel, perceive and behave when looking for personal fulfilment and community welfare. You need to consider:

- What is wrong?
- What is right?
- Am I satisfied with how I behave?

Development of an ethical identity: this means that you have become the author of your own life. It includes evaluating and decision-making skills.

5

Consider this scenario:

CAS SNAPSHOT

A group of students are going to Cambodia to work on a classroom-building project in a village. Without the money raised from your school the project will not go ahead. At the end of the three-week trip, you will all visit ancient temples and make a boat-trip down a river.

When you arrive, one student says that she was only really interested in coming on the trip because she wanted to make the visits to the temples, and that she lied about her motives for coming on the trip when she was interviewed for her place. She boasts that she will try to avoid doing as much of the work as possible as she really does not want to get to dirty. Moreover, she is critical of several other students on the trip. She also texts her parents complaining about the standard of the hotel you are staying in.

Some questions for you to consider:

1. How should you deal with your colleague?

2. What responsibilities do you have to the teachers that have organised this particular trip?

3. How do you deal with your own feelings towards this student who has been a good friend to you?

Figure 5.3 School children in Cambodia.

114

Some questions on ethics.

1   You have an opportunity to be awarded a penalty in a football match when a defender sticks out a leg. What do you do? Dive?

2   You are due to play for your hockey team, but you go to a party the night before. Do you stay until the party finishes, or leave early?

3   On Saturday morning you are expected to go to a soup kitchen. However, a friend calls you and asks if you want to go water-skiing. What do you do?

4   You have to go to work at the old people's home after school and you don't want to have to play chess with the old man who keeps telling you the same stories each week. What do you do?

5   One of your classmates has not done any reflections for CAS and he asks if he can borrow your reflections to copy. What do you do: give him the reflections, or ignore his request?

6   You decide that for your CAS project that you are going to raise funds for a building project overseas. One of the other people involved keeps some of the money for himself. What do you do?

7   You discover that the charity you are raising money for is not spending the money as it says it would. What do you do?

Personal values are part of your ethical identity. The following activity allows you to explore your values.

You survive a shipwreck and land on a deserted island in the middle of the Indian Ocean. What things would you most value from this list?

1   A tent with groundsheet

2   A month's supply of canned food

3   A set of flares

4   Two large empty plastic containers (5 litres' capacity)

5   Matches

6   A person that you know but do not get on well with

7   A container with a complete wardrobe of new clothes

8   A radio

9   Your diary and a pen

10   A mirror

11   A sealed container of chocolate

12   Rope

Rate these items from the most important to the least. Compare the list with one that a classmate has made. What are the most important things to you? Why?

It is important to be clear about the things that you value most and not to be influenced in decision-making by others' opinions and values.

5.03 CAS and the other AOKs

So far we have looked at the link between ethics and CAS, and how ethical systems can help clarify our decision-making within CAS experiences and deepen the level at which we reflect about CAS experiences. Let's now take a look at some of the other AOKs in TOK, as they can also play a role in how we act in our CAS experiences.

Religious knowledge systems

This AOK examines the role that religion plays as we acquire knowledge. Religious knowledge may also affect the way that we act in a CAS experience. For example, questions that could be asked are:

1   To what extent have our own actions been governed by personal religious beliefs?

2   Have our actions been affected by stereotypes that we have of followers of a particular religious belief?

Indigenous knowledge

The scope of this knowledge framework is to explore knowledge which is specific to a particular culture or society, and look at how they acquire knowledge. Aborigines in Australia have a special relationship to the land that they live in, a spiritual relationship that fosters knowledge about their locality, that most other cultures do not have. If we work with indigenous people as part of our CAS experiences, we need to think about how that will influence their life.

Some questions based on this knowledge framework that could influence our CAS experiences and reflections include:

1   How much do we respect and value other cultural systems?

2   What knowledge have we gained of other cultures from interaction with them?

3   What is our role in developing and preserving indigenous cultures? To what extent is it worth preserving these cultures?

Human Sciences

The scope of this framework is to see how the Human Sciences (subjects within group three, 'individuals and societies') help us to gain knowledge. They are referred to as sciences because they use scientific method to test the validity of hypotheses. However, unlike the physical sciences, there are no laws in this discipline which have no exceptions to them.

Some questions or approaches that we could use here to help us carry out a CAS experience and/or reflect:

1   How representative have our investigations been in trying to find out the need for a service?

2   To what extent is it possible to obtain a reliable source of knowledge about a CAS experience?

3   To what extent is knowledge gained from an interview reliable?

Natural Sciences

The scope of this framework is to see how the Natural Sciences (Physics, Chemistry, Biology, Sport Sciences) help us to gain knowledge. The progression of science has been based on continual revision of observations of nature. Methodology is based around scientific method and trying to prove or disprove scientific laws (which are hard and fast rules with no exceptions).

5

Some questions that we could ask ourselves about planning a CAS experience or reflecting on it:

1   To what extent do we use the scientific method when using the CAS stages to plan a project?

2   To what extent can we develop hypotheses based on observations from our CAS experiences?

3   How is it possible to establish cause and effect relationships from CAS experiences?

Mathematics

The scope of mathematics is to be concerned with quantity, shape and size. Using mathematics we can create models of reality. All computer systems are based on mathematical algorithms. Mathematics relies heavily on reason to create a set of universal truths.

Some questions that might help us either to plan or reflect on a CAS activity using this knowledge area are:

1   To what extent can we find universal truths from experience?

2   To what extent can we use statistical evidence in deciding what action to take in a CAS project?

3   How much can we use analysis of trends in determining the needs of a community?

4   What type of mathematical data is useful to decide whether or not CAS projects have been beneficial to all the people involved in it?

History

The method used in History is to take information from a variety of different sources. The historian uses these different sources and some personal knowledge and imagination to interpret history.

Some questions that might help us to either plan or reflect on a CAS experience using this knowledge area:

1   How reliable is our own record of a CAS experience?

2   To what extent does bias affect our perception of a CAS experience?

3   How can we carry out service without the knowledge of the history of a community?

The Arts

The Arts embrace the following areas: Literature, Music, Visual Arts, Film, Dance and Theatre. They are concerned with defining what is Art, and the role that the Arts play in shaping different types of culture. Moreover, the Arts are also seen as a way of transforming society. The Arts offer many students the opportunity to have a creative experience in CAS.

Some questions that we might ask in planning CAS experiences or reflecting on them using a CAS experience:

1   How we can use our creative skills in carrying out service?

2   To what extent can we reflect on a CAS experience using a photograph, drawing or sketch?

3   To what extent can we find truth through creative experiences?

5.04 CAS and the TOK presentation

One of the formal pieces of assessment in the TOK is a presentation, which can be done individually or in a small group.

The presentation should:

- last up to 30 minutes for a small group (of three members, at the most)
- start with a real-life situation (that could be a CAS experience)
- pose a knowledge question derived from the real-life situation
- be linked with other real–life situations, which raise further knowledge questions
- involve analysis of the knowledge questions raised using the WOKs and relevant knowledge areas.

5

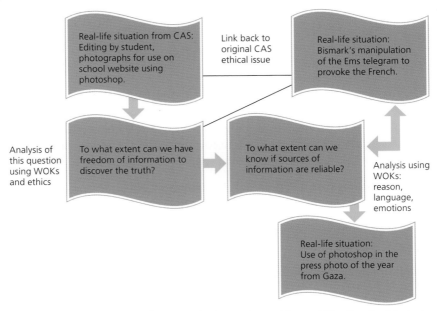

Figure 5.4 An example of using a CAS experience (the real-life situation) to help create a TOK presentation.

You can also plan your own TOK presentation based on an ethical situation from CAS.

Steps to follow in preparing a TOK presentation using a CAS experience as a starting point.

(I have used examples from Figure 5.4 to help you.)

1   You need to begin by choosing a CAS experience that involves you making ethical decision (the real-life situation in TOK terms).

In Figure 5.4: the real-life situation (the CAS experience) is the editing and censoring of student photography for the school yearbook. The students have been told to photoshop sports photos they have taken of students from other schools.

This is your real-life situation taken from your CAS experience.

2   You need to derive a knowledge question or questions based on this CAS experience.

As outlined above, these questions are open-ended (they cannot be answered with a 'yes' or 'no', and have a wide range of possible answers), are about knowledge, and often begin with a phrase or word such as: To what extent? How? How far?

An example of a knowledge question that could be derived from the situation in Figure 5.4 above is

'To what extent do we need to have freedom of information to know the truth?'

This is your knowledge question based on your real-life situation from CAS.

3   How are you going to analyse the knowledge question using WOKs and AOKs ?

From the example given above, we would consider using the AOK of ethics and also the role that sense-perception and reason might play in discussing this question.

Deciding which AOKs and WOKs you would use to analyse your knowledge question in step 2.

4   The knowledge question in step 3 should be related to a new real-life experience. From Figure 5.4, the following real-life situation could be taken from the area of the Arts. The press photograph of the year in 2013 was of a street scene in Gaza. However, there had been extensive photoshopping of the picture to alter the photo.

Deciding what real-life situation you would use that is related to your knowledge question in step 2.

5   You have to develop another knowledge question related to your original knowledge question in step 2. From the example in step 4, we could ask: 'To what extent can faith in art represent reality?' This could be analysed and discussed using the WOK of sense-perception and faith.

What would be your new knowledge question for your real-life situation for step 4?

6   You could look at another real-life issue from another AOK. A historical situation related to the manipulation of photographs is when Bismarck altered the telegram at Ems – a major factor which provoked the French into the Franco–Prussian war.

What would be your new real-life situation drawn from an AOK or CAS?

7   Link back to your original ethical issue based on a CAS experience.

Such an approach to the TOK presentation gives you a concrete starting place based on your own experiences. This makes the presentation more immediate and relevant to you. Be prepared to discuss some of the ethical issues you have faced with both your TOK teacher and CAS Coordinator or advisor. It is also important to clarify that your knowledge questions are strong ones with your TOK teacher.

Remember to make the presentation interesting and dynamic so that you engage your audience. It is perfectly reasonable to use drama, quizzes and audience participation to help reinforce and bring alive your arguments.

Key point: An important issue to remember is that you have free choice when preparing your TOK presentation, which helps you to narrow down your options. This section has been designed to show that CAS experiences can provide you with the material you need to create a high-standard TOK presentation.

5.05 CAS and the TOK essay

The TOK essay requires a different approach from the presentation because the IB provides you with a choice of topics that you have to choose from. Even so, there is always the chance to use your CAS experiences in the essay. Let us look at one of the topics for May 2015 that you could choose as a possible essay. This question has the potential to incorporate knowledge gained from CAS experiences. It must be stressed that while this is a good idea, it is not obligatory.

'The whole point of knowledge is to produce both meaning and purpose in our personal lives.'

To what extent do you agree with this statement?

Now let us look at a potential way of planning this essay.

1   A good starting point is to examine the knowledge claim that is inferred by the statement in the question.

What evidence do we have that this is true? Some questions we might ask ourselves about personal and shared knowledge:

- How often have we had to fail or suffer in order to gain important personal knowledge for ourselves?
- How different is the knowledge about a social problem provided by a great novel from knowledge gained by ourselves through experience?

First-hand knowledge is very important but we may not necessarily gain other perspectives from this; novels and good films can take us to the inner-feelings and life experiences of others in a very effective and safe way.

2 Evidence from personal and shared knowledge from CAS.

The knowledge that you would gain from working in a soup kitchen would give you both personal and shared knowledge about poverty in a city. The personal knowledge would come from your perceptions and memory of events, while shared knowledge would come through anecdotal conversations with the clients at the soup kitchen and from the managerial staff. This experience would also clarify some personal values about helping others that are less fortunate than ourselves.

3 Link to WOKs and some knowledge questions coming from this.

The WOK of sense-perception helps us to receive knowledge from this real-life situation. It is from our personal observations that we frame knowledge about both poor people and their lifestyle. Emotion (empathy or just experiencing other feelings toward what is seen) and reason also play a part in analysing the causes of the social context.

Knowledge questions that we could ask about this are:
- To what extent can our senses provide us with reliable information?
- Does emotion provide a unique knowledge in this situation?

In regards to memory, in this context you are relying heavily on your memory to recount knowledge that you have gleaned from the clients and management of this soup kitchen. A knowledge question that might be based on this:
- How far can we rely on our memories for valid knowledge?

4 Link to a knowledge area

For example, History. As discussed above, historians gather information from a variety of different sources then, using some personal knowledge and imagination, construct a narrative that provides an interpretation of history.

A knowledge question that might be based on this:
- How reliable is the knowledge gained from an eyewitness to an event?

Real-life situation: the use of eyewitness reports on the bombing of the German city of Dresden at the end of the Second World War in 1945 suggested that the loss of life was much greater than it actually was. Some wild estimates of 250 000 people being affected by the bombing were made by witness reports. However these reports were very useful in giving a picture of the impact of the fire bombing of the city, and the local response to what happened and some of the horrors that people endured.

This would provide us with an opportunity to analyse this research question, using the WOKs of memory and sense perception.

5 Link to other AOKs.

Ethics: The focal point of ethics is to decided whether or not our actions are moral or not. In doing this we need to analyse behaviour using the systems of ethics, which were described earlier in this chapter.

A knowledge question that could be asked is:
- To what extent can we justify human suffering if it is for the overall good?

Real-life situation: this could be related to the decision to bomb Dresden, mentioned above. Many historians have argued that it was unnecessary and a wanton destruction of a beautiful city, and an act of revenge, while others have argued that Dresden was a legitimate military target and its destruction helped to shorten the war, saving soldiers' lives.

6 Link back to the original question.

The TOK essay requires careful thought and planning:

1 You must engage with the question, identifying knowledge claims in the question and a possible knowledge question.

2 Maintain focus on the knowledge questions throughout the essay.

3 Consider knowledge questions in different AOKs and WOKs throughout the essay.

4 Consider the knowledge questions from different perspectives (claim and counterclaim).

5   Support your arguments with examples from real-life situations.

6   Each paragraph should have a clear point that it is making and should relate to the knowledge question. There should be evidence to support your arguments.

7   The voice of the knower should be heard throughout the essay. This occurs when you think how your own experiences as an IB student may have changed the way you see things, and when you question the knowledge that you have gained and how you have gained it.

Now it is your turn to plan a TOK essay that incorporates a CAS experience.

ACTIVITY BOX

From May 2015 there will be another TOK essay topic to explore:

'Ways of knowing are a check on our instinctive judgments.' To what extent do you agree with this statement?

1   What is the knowledge claim from this statement?
2   List evidence that you have from your CAS personal experience.
3   Link to WOKs and knowledge questions derived from this.
4   Link to AOKs:
   • real-life situation from knowledge area
   • knowledge questions derived from this real-life situation.
5   Link to other knowledge areas:
   • knowledge area
   • real-life situation related to this knowledge area
   • knowledge questions derived from this knowledge area.
6   Link back to original question.

Remember that this is being presented as a possible option for writing your TOK essay; you must choose the TOK essay topic that you feel most comfortable with.

5

Here are some other examples of prescribed TOK titles related to CAS.

1   Compare and contrast knowledge which can be expressed in words/
    symbols with knowledge that cannot be expressed in this way.
    Consider CAS and one or more areas of knowledge (November
    2011/May 2012).

2   As an IB student, how has your learning of literature and science
    contributed to your understanding of individuals and societies?
    (November 2011/May 2012)

    (*You could also consider referring to CAS as a way of understanding
    individuals and societies.*)

3   Using History and at least one other area of knowledge, examine the
    claim that it is possible to attain knowledge despite problems of bias
    and selection. (November 2011/May 2012)

    (*CAS experiences could be an example of how, despite initial bias, one
    can learn more about individuals and societies. Areas of knowledge are not
    separate, limited boxes of knowledge.*)

4   Some experts (such as athletes, dancers, musicians, visual artists, cabinet-
    makers, lab technicians, mechanics, surgeons) may have acquired
    knowledge that is difficult to describe in words. Does this mean the
    other Ways of Knowing play a more important role than language in
    knowing how to do something? (November 2006/ May 2007)

5   Are reason and emotion equally necessary in justifying moral
    decisions? (November 2007/May 2008)

    (*Ethical learning is not just a matter of rational analysis; it is also an
    emotional experiential learning.*)

6   'Moral wisdom seems to be as little connected to knowledge of
    ethical theory as playing good tennis is to knowledge of physics.'
    (Emrys Westacott) To what extent should our actions be guided by
    theories in ethics and elsewhere? (November 2008/May 2009)

5.06 CAS and the extended essay

The extended essay is a compulsory requirement where you choose a topic to research within an academic discipline. You are required to write an essay of 4 000 words, and it should be a piece of genuine research. A CAS experience or project could be the stimulus for an extended essay within a discipline.

Students often come across really interesting issues when carrying out a CAS experience or project. For example, if you are involved in an environmental group that is helping to preserve the ecology of a local area by helping to weed the area so that the native plants can survive, you may notice that some plants are only found on wet soil. A consequence could be to have an extended essay in Biology examining the relationship between soil type and plants.

Alternatively, one of your CAS experiences could be helping to run and lead a committee at a Model United Nations on nuclear proliferation. The hot issues that you discuss are whether or not all countries should be allowed to produce nuclear power, and how nuclear waste is disposed of. This experience could lead you to write an essay in world politics on the role of the UN.

The following CAS Snapshot provides an example of a student using their CAS involvement directly in their extended essay. You can see here how CAS not only gave inspiration for the topic, but also how the two core areas complemented each other for mutual gain.

CAS SNAPSHOT

NIST International School in Bangkok has been involved in an ongoing CAS project in Northern Thailand, working in areas including access to safe water supply, sanitation, solar lamps and provision of educational supplies. It was involvement in this project that led NIST student Jeffrey McLean to his extended essay topic and research question. Here are some comments from Jeffrey about the role of CAS in developing his ideas for his extended essay.

5

'Out of the five aspects our Maeramit CAS project was focusing on, sanitation intrigued me most.

- Sanitation related to my aspirations – to do something related to health and medicine.

- Out of my Diploma Programme subjects, I was most interested in doing an EE on Geography.

- Food and health was one of the units in the Geography syllabus, which clearly established the connection between my CAS activity and my coursework.

- Fieldwork is a requirement for Geography-based EE, and gathering data that combined parts of my CAS project and my EE was a very attractive idea because I would be able to "bring more to the table" for the CAS project due to my greater knowledge from the research I had done for the extended essay. I could also use my prolonged involvement in the CAS project to bring my extended essay to life.

It was clear that both my CAS and my EE benefited from being on the same topic – so there was no looking back!'

Jeffrey, NIST International School

Figure 5.5 Students conducting activities in a needs analysis in Northern Thailand.

Let us look at some CAS experiences and the links they might have to an extended essay.

CAS experience	Extended essay topic	Discipline
Helping to remove rubbish that has been dumped in a stream	An examination of water purity in a stream	Chemistry
Working on a nature reserve to ensure that it is not overrun with invasive species	A survey of the native plants in the nature reserve and the soil conditions they need	Biology
Helping to re-vegetate a ski slope	A survey of the relationship between soil depth and plant growth	Environmental Systems
Working with old people	Oral History project on a topic that one of the residents has some experience of	History
Working with a small charity	Examining the business plan for the charity	Business and Management
Reading for the blind	This leads to a literature essay comparing the styles of two authors that you have read	Language A
Working with street children	Looking at the migration patterns of street children	Geography

Now it is your turn to think about possible extended essay topics from CAS experiences.

ACTIVITY BOX

Complete the table with thoughts about how your CAS experiences or project could lead to an extended essay.

CAS experience	Possible topic	Discipline

5

5.07 CAS and the World Studies extended essay

A world studies extended essay must focus on a topic of global significance … The student should then explore how their chosen issue may be illustrated in a local context or contexts using specific examples of a small scale, local phenomenon; in this way the student is linking the local to the global.

As the approach is interdisciplinary explaining the topic through the lens of more than one discipline, students should develop a clear rationale for taking an interdisciplinary approach, selecting the IB disciplines through which they plan to explore the topic.

*www.ibo.org/en/programmes/diploma-programme/curriculum/
extended-essay/world-studies/, IBO, June 2015).*

The *Extended Essay Guide* (2013) indicates the following global issues could be considered:

- language, culture and identity
- science, technology and society
- equality and inequality
- conflict, peace and security
- economic and/or environmental sustainability
- health and development.

One of the CAS learning outcomes is to demonstrate engagement with issues of global significance. The following activity considers the connections between some CAS experiences and these issues.

ACTIVITY BOX

Complete this table looking at CAS experiences and their global significance.

CAS experience	Issue of global significance
Working with migrants, teaching them the local language	
Helping to clean up a beach area and preserve a coastal foreshore	
	Education of all children
	Global warming

The extended essay for World Studies has to meet the following requirements:

1 It is grounded in two disciplines (a hint from the 2013 Extended Essay Report: the most successful essays were those that were based on issues from two very different disciplines, such as Language and Geography).

2 It must show the relationship between the issues at a local level and a global level (this where a CAS experience may be valuable).

3 It must fulfil the basic requirements of an extended essay in any subject (maximum of 4000 words in length, including an abstract, introduction, conclusion, referencing of sources and listing of all sources used).

If you write a World Studies extended essay, you are advised to keep a reflective journal so that you can consider the global issue that you are engaged with and see how it helps you to see your own role as a global citizen. It is important that you make this connection between what is going on at a local level and the bigger global picture. Often, the only place that you regularly encounter a global issue is through a CAS experience, particularly in the area of service. While it might appear that helping at an old people's home is a local service, caring for the elderly is increasingly becoming a significant problem in every developed country. This may lead to examining the issue from a geographical viewpoint (the demography) or a psychological viewpoint (looking at altruism in volunteering).

It is making this connection between your experience, a global issue and academic study that is a real challenge. You may be helped in making this connection if your school chooses a service learning approach to CAS, where links are made between the subjects and CAS (see Chapter 4).

5

5.08 Review of Chapter 5

1   What are the three key aims of coherence that bond TOK, CAS and the extended essays together?

2   What are main sources of knowledge for both TOK and CAS?

3   What are the different ethical systems? How are ethics relevant to decision-making in CAS experiences?

4   How do TOK skills help CAS reflections?

5   In what ways can CAS experiences inform a TOK presentation or essay?

6   How can CAS provide the stimulus for an extended essay?

7   What is the link between the World Studies extended essay and CAS?

5.09 A summary of this chapter

This chapter has covered the following points:

- An explanation of the relationship between CAS and TOK, and CAS and the Extended Essay
- The link between TOK and CAS (how we gain knowledge from CAS experiences)
- How CAS experiences can lead to TOK knowledge claims and questions
- WOKs to help deepen reflection in CAS
- Questions about ethical situations in CAS that highlight the relationship between the AOK of ethics and CAS
- How to use a CAS experience for both a TOK presentation and essay, with some examples provided
- How to use a CAS experience as basis for a World Studies extended essay.

CAS projects

6

How would you define the word 'project'? Words that come to mind might include 'a significant task', 'a major undertaking', 'a venture completed over time' or 'a task involving planning to fulfil a particular goal'. These terms provide us with a glimpse of what the topic of this chapter – the CAS project – is about.

It would be highly likely that 'projects' have been referred to by you or your teachers when talking about previous learning tasks. This chapter will explore the nature of projects in CAS. We will start by outlining the expectations surrounding your involvement in CAS projects. We will then focus on CAS project methodology, looking at how the CAS stages are to be used, and provide some resources to help you in finding, planning and implementing your CAS projects. Examples of CAS projects in the different strands of CAS will also be presented.

> **A CAS project:** is a 'collaborative, well-considered series of sequential CAS experiences, engaging students in one or more of the CAS strands of creativity, activity, and service'. *CAS Guide* (2015), page 24, IBO

Have you previously been given an assignment that your teacher called a 'project'? If so, how did it differ from other tasks? What school projects have you been involved in?

6.01 What is involved in a CAS project?

You are expected to become involved in at least one CAS project during your CAS programme. Let us now explore the definition of a CAS project from the *CAS Guide*, as this will help you understand what you are expected to undertake in your CAS projects.

'Collaborative'

You are required to work with others in the planning, delivery and evaluation of your projects. This can be with a partner or a larger group, and may involve collaborating with other students from your school or another school, or with members of the wider community. Whatever the size of your group and where members are from, everyone should play an active role in all stages of the project. The roles that various members play should be clearly defined in your action plan, which is developed during the Preparation stage of your projects.

'Well-considered'

This refers to the thought and planning that is required in your project. All CAS projects should use the CAS stages as a framework, and as we have seen in Chapter 2, much work is required before you can go ahead and act. Because your project is expected to be a significant undertaking, the duration and complexity of the Investigation and Preparation stages are likely to be at a higher level than in a CAS experience. Planning (and implementing) a sustained CAS project provides opportunities to enhance and integrate your personal interests, skills and talents into your collaborative work, and to demonstrate a number of the CAS learning outcomes.

Key point: Words that should describe your CAS project include: significant, sustained, meaningful, important, ongoing, notable, well-planned, purposeful, committed.

'Series of sequential CAS experiences'

A CAS project can be based in any one of the three CAS strands, or be a combination of two or all three strands. Whichever area of CAS the project is based in, a minimum of one month's duration is recommended, although CAS projects of longer duration can provide greater opportunities for all participants. A project that lasts for four weeks, from the first involvement of investigation to the final action, generally means that your commitment and contributions are intense, something that can be quite stressful. Wherever possible, it is suggested that your project take place with regular commitment over a longer period of time. In addition to collaboration, it is the prolonged commitment that helps to differentiate between a CAS experience and a CAS project.

Take a look at the following CAS Snapshot and consider how the three elements of the CAS 'project' definition might be seen.

6

CAS SNAPSHOT

'My project began where another CAS experience finished. I was involved in delivering a reading comprehension programme at a local school, Santa Rosa de Llanavilla in Peru, where other CAS students and I read books and conducted activities for the children there. This included planning creative role-playing of the stories to develop comprehension skills in a more didactic way. It was when our lessons finished that I decided to build a small library in Llanavilla School; and luckily some of my friends decided to join me in this project.

'So we worked as a community, raising funds to purchase building supplies, then using our own hands to transform the bricks and mortar into a functioning library – an opportunity to take steps in improving literacy in this area of Peru. Raising the money to make this possible was, for us, something that we have never done before: we learnt how to be good at sales. Even with our lack of sales experience, our team succeeded in running two small 'businesses' for fund-raising. Then there was the construction. It is not until you face the reality of building, that you realise how hard it is. Activities included carrying half of my body weight in bags full of sand, learning how to build a wall and learning how to paint everything in both theory and practise.

'Having finished the project, I have some advice for CAS students on how to be involved in a successful CAS project: do something that makes you happy, that will make you learn, something that allows you to escape your comfort zone; and something where you show perseverance and personal commitment. Not just because CAS requires so, but for your own self-respect and because the people you are helping deserve it. Building the library was not easy at all. We worked for hours in the heat, building and painting after weeks and weeks of raising funds. It wasn't simple, but in the end that persistence becomes satisfaction and commitment becomes pride.'

Jorge, Colegio San Agustín, Lima.

Figure 6.1 Students from Colegio San Agustin pulling building materials up to the building site for the library.

This snapshot shows regular participation and collaboration over a significant period of time. You can see that innovation and initiative were also involved, and elements of the CAS stages are evident. On top of this, the snapshot also demonstrates passion, enjoyment and learning – points that can make CAS projects all the more beneficial.

Prolonged commitment to a project provides opportunities for you to show initiative, demonstrate perseverance and be a critical thinker. Your involvement can also help develop problem-solving, interpersonal and decision-making skills. This significant engagement provides scope for personal growth as well as evidence of achievement in the CAS learning outcomes. Being involved in a project team promotes experiential learning, with people working and learning together while sharing points of view, perspectives and awareness of each other's feelings. All participants in the project team need to contribute while encouraging and respecting the contributions of others. So as you can see, the CAS project offers you many benefits!

It is important to highlight that by its very nature, the CAS project largely depends on your motivation and commitment. Actively attending planning sessions, participating in regular meetings and turning up to each session when you are in the Action stage requires your dedication and perseverance. Though your CAS Coordinator, your parents or other members of your group may give encouragement, this really needs to come from you. You are the protagonist of your own learning!

What can help you and other members of the CAS project group to stay motivated in your work?

Key point: The principal objective of the CAS project is to see Diploma students involved in sustained collaboration.

Relevance plays a big role in the success of your project. It is much easier to commit to something when you can see its purpose. Extending this, regular participation in your project becomes something you look forward to when it is relevant, and you enjoy doing it! This is why it is very important that you thoroughly investigate your options when it comes to commencing a project – use this CAS stage to consider what you want to do, where your interests lie, what opportunities there are, and what talents you have. As the project must involve collaboration, it is wise to discuss these points with the people you know, so that you can explore opportunities you could jointly get involved in, keeping in mind that it is your choice; you get to decide what you want to do for your project!

6

Now let's do an exercise that can help you answer the question – what is the difference between a CAS experience and a CAS project?

To help you distinguish between a CAS project and a CAS experience, pay attention to:

1 Who is involved: acting alone would mean that it is an experience. Joining with others could make it into a project.

2 The nature of the involvement: attendance without much influence on decision-making or the direction of the pursuit would mean that it is an experience. Being involved with others in making decisions and planning for your action could mean that it is a project.

3 The degree or length of your involvement: short-term engagement would probably make this an experience. Regular involvement over a number of weeks or months may mean that it is a project.

Table 6.1 provides CAS experiences in the middle column and CAS projects on the right-hand column, based on a particular pursuit or topic. Fill in the empty boxes, using the points above, and note the difference between a CAS experience and a CAS project. The first few rows are completed for you.

Topic/pursuit	A CAS experience	A CAS project
Basketball	Being a player in the school basketball team over an 8-week season.	Organizing a 3-on-3 basketball competition open to entries from all high schools in the district, held over two days in the school gym, with prize money for the winning team donated by sponsors.
Music	Learning the guitar, aiming to be able to play five songs within three months.	Writing original songs with your band, aiming to record them and produce an album.
Teaching	Support younger students in preparing for a Model UN conference in a month's time.	With support from an NGO working in the topic, plan and deliver a curriculum with your group for a literacy programme for local children.

Handball		Recruit fellow students and friends to form a team to enter a local tournament. Work together to organise weekly skill and fitness training sessions over the 12-week season.
Environmental stewardship		Organise an awareness and fund-raising event for an organisation protecting local wildlife.
Film	Make a one-minute clip using flash animation.	
Writing	Write an article for a local monthly magazine.	
Supporting disadvantaged children		

Table 6.1

6.02 Project methodology – the CAS stages

The CAS stages are to be followed when you carry out your CAS project. Chapter 2 of this book contains ideas and resources that you could use to guide you in the various CAS stages to plan, implement and evaluate your CAS projects. This chapter will add to those activities and ideas.

CAS projects obviously involve project-based learning, an educational methodology that has been implemented all around the world. From the very start of your involvement, project-based learning encourages your ownership of the process, for you and other members of your CAS project.

Project-based learning: focused on real-life situations and challenges, and relies on investigation, decision-making and problem-solving skills.

As outlined above, CAS projects must involve collaboration. This in itself adds an additional dimension to the CAS stages – you need to approach the different tasks within each stage with other project members. Additionally, as

6

you progress through the CAS stages you need to ensure that your proposed ideas adhere to the expectations of a CAS project listed above – the project must be well-considered and allow for sustained collaboration.

Before looking at how the CAS stages can be applied in CAS projects, take a look at the following CAS Snapshot – can you spot tasks completed in the different CAS stages in this brief outline?

CAS SNAPSHOT

Kiva project

'Kiva is a non-profit organisation that aims to aid and alleviate poverty by providing microloans to aspiring entrepreneurs in underdeveloped countries. They focus on providing opportunities to people who are prepared to work hard to achieve their goals and beat poverty. To me, the most important aspect of the organisation and a key reason for getting involved with them is that we can help people in need by giving them the opportunity to fight for their economic stability in their own way.

'When I first started the Diploma Programme, I had an immediate interest in creating support for KIVA. After talking to some friends that also showed interest, I met the school's CAS Coordinator and presented our project idea. There were some initial concerns about setting up accounts and our beneficiaries being able to repay loans. After further investigation, we came up with more considered proposals that were then approved by the school.

'To commence the Kiva club, we gathered everyone involved and developed our goals. We separated into two groups, one focusing on the creation of the bank account in order to gather and distribute funds as well as increasing our profile as a school group, while the other group focused on an initial fund-raising project. We managed to raise some funds to start up the loans, and are currently in the process of working with benefactors and supporting their loan applications. We set up a data bank of companies, groups and individuals we will approach to support the project, and have developed some proposals that will be presented to possible donors.

'It is challenging but rewarding to be involved in this club. We are involved in complex issues such as developing our funds and then selecting the projects and people to support that we feel will best benefit the community. This requires much review and research, and discussion among our group. We review the reliability of the partners and also the social impact that each dollar will provide. It is a difficult task, but I am looking forward to seeing how the project evolves!'

Andres, International School Nido de Aguilas, Santiago de Chile.

Investigation

As your project could involve you joining an existing project, your investigation should explore what projects are currently being conducted that you may have access to. This includes clubs or groups in your school or local community. Consider also online projects you may get involved in. You do not need to establish a project, but your CAS project must offer you the chance to be involved in Investigation and Preparation, together with other members of the group. As CAS projects involve collaboration, you also need to investigate who you could work with.

> **Key point:** You are not required to initiate a CAS project, but your CAS project should clearly offer the opportunity to engage in all of the CAS stages.

Once your ideas for the project are clear, the Investigation stage then involves collecting materials and information from people, newspapers, libraries, experts, external organisations and more. Also conduct an audit of your group, highlighting any special skills and knowledge that group members may have that could be used in planning and implementing your project. Useful tools in your investigation include interviews, observations and questionnaires. Refer to Chapter 2 section 2.01 and also Chapter 4 section 4.04 for more details on this.

If your project is service-based, the investigation must involve your group exploring the various opportunities for you to engage in your community and making connections with people in the community you wish to work with. Chapter 4 on service learning provides more details on this – when you look at the ideas and resources outlined there, do keep in mind that all members of your group need to be involved in conducting the various aspects of your project investigation.

The following CAS Snapshot provides an example of aspects of the Investigation stage conducted by students in Thailand. Conducting a needs analysis, an important part of the Investigation stage of service, can be seen in this example.

> **Needs analysis:** a technique used to gather information about the needs of a community or group, focusing on the issues or problems faced in that group. The needs refer to gaps or areas of concern; things that are needed to help better support that community.

6

CAS CASE STUDY

Investigation – conducting a needs analysis

After hearing about the possibilities of establishing a CAS project in Maeramit village in Northern Thailand, students at NIST International School, Bangkok saw the importance of investigating and confirming the needs of this community first-hand.

The first NIST students to visit the village knew very little about it. Over a period of three nights in the village, the students completed a comprehensive needs analysis of the village and its surroundings. This included walking around the village, observing and making basic maps, and expanded into the creation of a calendar of village daily and seasonal life, an inventory of assets and a series of interviews with local people.

The next step was to have formal meetings with various groups of villagers such as children, women, and men to find out about their life and development needs. Staying in the village, experiencing the basic conditions with limited electricity and sanitation facilities, was an investigation itself into what it was like to live in Maeramit. This also helped to create a relationship with the local population and empathy towards them, which consequently became a strong motivator for driving the project.

The final stage was a community meeting where NIST students facilitated a session to determine the top five development needs of the village. These have become the focus of the development projects the students are working on as part of their CAS.

Figure 6.2 A NIST International School student involved in a needs analysis as a part of the Investigation stage.

Preparation

With collaboration being a key element of the CAS project, the Preparation stage for your project must involve your group working together to assign roles for each team member. All members of the project team should be involved in developing the plan, and tasks should be shared among all team members so that they are equal participants when taking action.

Together with your team you need to develop your aims and objectives, establish the scope and possible limitations of your plans, clarify roles and responsibilities, determine resources and timelines, and identify and acquire any skills needed to engage in the project.

6

Use this table with your group to establish and develop your project ideas.

1. WHAT? Nature of the project	
2. WHY? Rationale	
3. WHAT FOR? Aims, objectives, purposes	
4. HOW LONG? Scope	
5. WHERE? Physical setting, location	
6. HOW? Activities, methodology	
7. WHEN? Schedule, timelines	
8. WITH WHOM? Group members, and in the case of a service project, target population	
9. WHO? Human resources	
10. WITH WHAT? Material resources	

Action

Your action plan should aim for all group members to be active contributors to your project. As such, each team member should have a clear idea of their role in addition to knowing where/how to access resources that may support them in fulfilling their responsibilities. Your Preparation stage should have involved your group members in 'up-skilling' themselves so that they are prepared to take action in completing their tasks.

SPOTLIGHT ON ... COLLABORATION

Like all CAS involvement, CAS projects allow for learning through experience. Participating in a project provides opportunities to increase self-awareness, promotes open-mindedness and interpersonal understanding and can facilitate decision-making and problem-solving skills. Additionally, as the CAS project requires collaboration, it also promotes communication skills, requiring you to be involved in negotiation, agreements and consensus. Involvement in a CAS project provides an opportunity for shared learning – for you and other group members to construct meaning from your CAS involvement. Working closely with others exposes you to other perspectives and points of view, to engage in discussion that can facilitate critical reflection, and develop conflict resolution and listening skills. You may also learn about commitment to group goals and respect for agreements, and gain first-hand experience of leadership skills.

Reflection

Reflection should be ongoing, occurring at all stages of your CAS project. As your project involves working with others, you should create opportunities where you can reflect together with other members of the group as this would best support your CAS project reflections. Whether it is led by the project supervisor, CAS Coordinator or even one of your fellow group members, group reflections allow you to hear and respond to the thoughts, feelings and ideas of others. This can guide you to reflecting at a deeper level. Chapter 3 provides some ideas for group reflection activities, and the activity below contains more suggestions.

Key point: Reflecting with others can introduce you to different perspectives and enable you to reflect on a deeper level.

6

Pass the reflection
This exercise can be done with any item belonging to somebody in the group. Start with a group member holding the item, and sharing a reflection with the group. They then pass the item to the next person. Continue until all members have shared their reflections.

News report
Working in smaller groups or pairs, group members take it in turns to role-play a news reporter reporting on the project that day or that month.

Pass the sentence
Somebody in the group starts with a sentence about the project. He or she then passes the story onto the next person, who continues with a sentence and then passes it on.

Word of the day
Each group member provides one or two words to describe his or her involvement in the project that day or up until that moment.

Four corners
A statement or question is presented to the group about the project and their thoughts or feelings about it. In response to the statement/question, group members move to a corner designated as Strongly Agree, Agree, Neutral, Disagree and Strongly Disagree. Neutral could also be added in the middle of the areas. Request individual members to elaborate on why they chose where to stand.

Symbols
Ask members of the group to name something that symbolises how they are feeling or what they are thinking about the project.

Read all about it
Group members provide a headline to a newspaper article that represents something about their involvement in the project.

Somethings
Ask group members to finish these 'something' sentence stems:

Something I didn't know before is ...
Something I would like to tell others is ...
Something that challenged (or is challenging) me ...
Something I need to do is ...

What factors may determine which of these group reflection activities you might try with your project group? What are some other methods you might use to encourage your CAS project group to reflect together?

Demonstration

Though you can individually showcase your CAS project in your CAS portfolio, CAS projects can also involve your team sharing this task. Your group could present the project to a school assembly or class, hold an information booth in your school during lunchtime or create a video clip and post it online. Having your group participate in a final shared reflection is also recommended, and could also involve an evaluation of your project. This is best approached when led by your project supervisor, and in the case of service projects it should also involve the community you are working with.

This CAS Snapshot provides an example of sharing and celebrating a CAS project in a public forum.

CAS SNAPSHOT

Demonstrating CAS at a TEDx event

DC Labour Rights is a student-run organisation founded by students at Hong Kong's Discovery College in 2012. The group is committed to making a change within labour rights globally, focusing on two main campaigns: the Blacklist campaign, which aimed to educate people about widespread labour issues, and the VTech campaign, an ongoing project that aims to improve the working conditions within a VTech factory in Dongguan, China.

The DC Labour Rights group was approached by students from Chinese University Hong Kong to speak at their TEDxCUHK event. Francesca Phillips, who represented the group, said that speaking at the event was an incredible experience: 'The TEDx talk felt like a demonstration of the efforts of the group over the past few years and it was fantastic to be able to promote education regarding labour issues. It was great to present alongside accomplished individuals and share how working in the group has been a really good opportunity to learn more about global issues and to collaborate with knowledgeable individuals.'

Participating in the event allowed the group to spread awareness of their efforts and goals, to share their successes, and to increase understanding about labour issues in the region. It also provided Francesca with a personal challenge and an opportunity to develop her public-speaking skills.

Figure 6.3   Demonstrating CAS at TEDxCUHK.

How could you demonstrate your CAS in a public forum? What opportunities are there in your local community to share your CAS efforts?

Before we move on to looking at CAS projects based in the different strands of CAS, or based in more than one strand, let's look at a proposal form that can be used to inform others about your project ideas.

ACTIVITY BOX

This form can be used as a framework for developing your CAS project proposal, which your CAS Coordinator may request. It could also function as an element of a grant or funding/donor proposal form. Completing this form will also assist with aspects of the Investigation and Preparation stages of CAS.

Project title _____

CAS strand of the project – (for projects including more than one strand, provide the relevance of each strand):

Creativity _____
Activity _____
Service _____

Project team member _____

Project contact person _____

Project supervisor _____

Project dates _____

Project outline
Provide an overview of your project and what you hope to achieve

```



```

Project goal/s
Keep in mind the SMART goal format – refer to Chapter 2 section 2.01

```



```

Investigation
List key areas that will require investigation

```

```

Project action plan
List the key tasks required to complete the project. Attach your action plan at the end of the proposal.

Key resources
List people/organisations that might be helpful in achieving your goals. Consider local NGOs and community groups, experts, and so on.

Project monitoring and evaluation
Describe how you will monitor progress and evaluate outcomes

6.03 Creativity projects

When thinking of Creativity CAS projects, you should think about those creative endeavours that you want to get involved in, or an interest to learn more about. Consider those areas of the traditional Arts, like learning to play an instrument, forming or joining a band, learning about photography, becoming a member of a theatre group, painting, undertaking a pottery course, dancing, signing. Consider also other areas that rely on creative thought, originality and innovation as their basis, such as designing a house using CAD software, creating a range of infographics, designing a range of fashion. There is a wide range of possibilities!

In section 6.01 we explored the differences between a CAS project and a CAS experience. When you are considering a CAS project in Creativity, you need to ensure that it offers scope for sufficient application of the CAS stages, and that it will enable you and other group members to be involved in sustained collaboration.

In this CAS Snapshot we see how a student's passion for theatre was used as the basis for a Creativity CAS project. We can also see the impact which participating in this CAS project had on this student.

CAS SNAPSHOT

Legally Blonde

'*Legally Blonde* was our school's 2013 theatre production. Over a period of four months we rehearsed twice a week, and then we held additional rehearsals as the dates of the production approached. I chose to get involved in this activity because I love theatre and I have never been involved in a musical before. I thought that it would be a good way to expand my experience and try a new style of theatre. I also love this particular musical, and thought it would be fun to get involved and meet new people in other classes who share my passion for theatre.

'Although this amazing project was time-consuming, I was really disappointed when it ended. It was a lot of fun to work on something that I am passionate about, and to do this with others who shared the same passion. One thing I realised from my involvement is that I am not very open with others when working in groups and cannot express my ideas clearly. I tried to develop this, working with different groups and offering my ideas and suggestions as much as I could, and trying to interact with people of different year levels to whom I had never spoken before.

'I only ever missed a single rehearsal, because I had a theatre lesson in which I learned skills of voice and projection, which was useful later in this production as I had to project my voice and portray my character through the use of voice (tone, pitch, key and so on). This was a really good experience for me: I developed as a theatre student, gained a lot of new social and technical skills, and really enjoyed all three performances.'

Clara, Discovery College, Hong Kong.

Figure 6.4 The cast of the production *Legally Blonde*, Discovery College.

6.04 Activity projects

The holistic approach of the IB Diploma Programme encourages you to develop as a whole person. A part of this is achieving a healthy lifestyle, balancing your academic and social pursuits with regular physical activity.

The CAS project provides an opportunity for you to get involved in planned, sustained exercise on a regular basis. This may be a sport or recreation at a level that you have not pursued before, or a physical challenge that may require months of preparation. Examples may include joining a partner or group to develop rock-climbing skills so that you can complete a class 5 graded climb; preparing for a half or full marathon; training for a 5 km ocean swim; conducting a personal fitness training programme; working to achieve a blue belt in karate; being a regular in the starting line-up of your school basketball team; or regular yoga to increase the difficulty in poses.

Activity projects should offer you the scope to get involved in all of the CAS stages – there needs to be an opportunity for Investigation and Preparation. This may involve designing training sessions, improving your knowledge so that you can be involved in creating conditioning programmes, organising practise sessions or gaining qualifications so that you can be involved in coaching and administration.

Like all CAS projects, there should be an element of being challenged through participating in an Activity project. The project you choose should offer an opportunity for personal growth and the potential for change. An Activity project therefore must not be just your regular involvement but something that will test your limits and inspire you to reach new boundaries. And, of course, Activity projects offer much opportunity for fun and enjoyment!

CAS SNAPSHOT

Project Adventure

'The IB programme has prepared me to go to university, taught me to follow my passions and question knowledge, and shown me that everyone can contribute something to society. However CAS has taught me to be brave, and my involvement in Project Adventure taught me to take risks, trust other people and open my mind to new activities which, a year before, I would never thought possible.

'As a child, I never had a fear of trying new things; I took risks, and didn't think about them. My childhood was filled with canoe trips in the summer, skiing in the winter and Sunday hikes. But as I got older I lost interest in these activities, and as with many other aspects in life, I was scared to do it again after so many years. Project Adventure made me look back at my childhood and integrate those experiences into my adult life. I managed to overlook the fear of failing and looking stupid; I could finally look past my own pre-judgement.

'At my school we had a Project Adventure CAS club in which a group of students learnt about outdoor adventure experiences. It was an opportunity to gain skills and knowledge in order to plan and participate in activities such as climbing, ice climbing, skiing and hiking. It was fantastic to be in nature once again!

'My learning curve for the first couple of months of climbing was steep, but when I got more advanced, climbing suddenly became much more serious than the playful game I was used to. I started lead-climbing on bolts; it felt reasonably fine and I continued doing this for a long while before I tried lead-climbing with traditional gear. This stopped me, and suddenly all lead-climbing became too challenging and too terrifying. I was afraid of falling and hurting myself. The fear found a way in and became a self-fulfilling prophecy – I was scared of falling, and so fell. Then I was scared of trusting my own judgement. The fact that I was not used to being scared only made it worse and harder to overcome. Nonetheless, the more I climbed the better it felt. It took a long time to overcome this fear and it is still something I work on whenever I go climbing.

'But because I overcame this fear I could push myself to even greater heights! I can now ski steeper slopes, undertake harder climbs and take greater risks. I am stronger, not only physically but also mentally. This mental strength has helped me in my personal life too, and it is easier for me now to take on new challenges, whether it is a new job or the new country in which I live. These activities have given me new friends, a new hobby and most importantly a better quality of life.'

Anna, Skagerak, Norway.

6

6.05 Service projects

Service in CAS promotes a real commitment to human and social development, with the aim of helping 'to create a better and more peaceful world' (IB Mission Statement) for everybody. It refers to the learning process through community engagement and generates a social responsibility that can be put into action.

Service experiences allow you to push yourself to meet others in need and to do something concrete at improving their life conditions. In doing so it is essential that your attitudes and actions are respectful of those you are working with, and that you understand that everybody has something valuable to give and receive.

Our next CAS snapshot provides us with an example of a service-based CAS project. It clearly outlines activities completed in the CAS stages by the students involved.

CAS SNAPSHOT

Center of Adaptation of Youth CAS Project, Nazarbayev Intellectual School of Astana (NISA), Kazakhstan

This project involved students from Nazarbayev Intellectual School of Astana (NISA) working with the Center of Adaptation of Youth (CAY), a place that houses and cares for children whose parents are unable to look after them due to different social issues. Children from CAY visit NISA's campus once a week to participate in various sporting competitions and games. In this way the students from the Center get the chance to have fun and enjoy some time in the company of other members of the community.

Investigation

Following connections and initial visits made by the school's CAS Coordinators, students visited the Center a few times to meet some of the children and explore the kind of support they needed. After hearing the opinions and expectations of the CAY children and talking to the Center's administrators, plans were developed about the kind of activities the students could organise for the children, and goals for the project were drawn up. The initial visits also provided an opportunity for NISA students to interact with the children and discover their own skills and abilities in relating to them.

Preparation

Initial preparation involved developing some skills in leading activities for the children, and the group divided into subgroups to plan activities targeted at different ages after it was identified that different age groups could attend each week without notice. Students returned to the Preparation stage to further develop their plans, adding ice-breaker activities as every week there would be a different set of children attending. A need to keep the balance of games suitable for both boys and girls was also identified, so the plans were revised again. There was also a need for some conflict resolution activities, and NISA students attended meetings with the school psychologist who helped them to develop techniques on conflict prevention and management.

Action

Weekly plans are developed by the NISA students and, following approval, are taught to the children on their weekly visits. The nature of the project means that clear evidence is produced for most of the CAS learning outcomes.

Reflection

Here is an excerpt from a student's reflection:

'After a while of being involved, I have become closer to the children and I truly fell in love with every child. After consulting with a psychologist, we began to work with more than one whole group, and in small groups according to their interests and age. Now it is easier to work with them and I look forward to our lessons. We have already played almost all the games and we have lots of fun. Now, after getting to know each child personally, I know how to behave around different children. At the moment, we are playing different games with them like small competitions in football, volleyball and other games that we created. The most important thing I have learnt on this project is to find a common language with people. I realised that if you show love to the child, then he will also love you.'

Sara

Figure 6.5   Planning and delivering a youth programme as a part of CAS.

6.06 Projects combining two or three of the CAS strands

It is important not to consider the CAS strands as mutually exclusive. Many times they are interwoven.

You can combine Creativity and Activity; Creativity and Service; Activity and Service or all three strands in a single project; the *CAS Guide* (2015, page 24) is clear on this point:

A CAS project can address any single strand of CAS, or combine two or all three strands.

You may find that this interaction of CAS strands will significantly contribute to getting the most out of a CAS project. As we always say: the whole of CAS is greater than the sum of its parts!

This next CAS Case Study highlights how Creativity can be combined with Action through choreographing and rehearsing a dance production.

CAS CASE STUDY

Dance project 'Reverie'

Reverie was a dance project conceived, choreographed and performed by students of the Dover campus at United World College of South East Asia. Students Phoebe Wang and Katrina Gunara led a student team working over a number of months on the project that culminated with three sold-out performance nights.

After developing some initial concepts, students undertook the planning of logistics such as dates for auditions and the shows, and budgets. Auditions for choreographers and dancers were held, which led to the selection of the team that would be choreographing and rehearsing over a number of months to prepare for the show. The project gave performers an opportunity to collaborate creatively, and required many hours of rehearsal to physically prepare for the production.

Putting the production together involved a number of different tasks. While the on-stage performances were being prepared for, promotional material and stage design were required. Promotional flyers and banners were created, sets were designed and dress rehearsals were organised, with many obstacles overcome in the process! According to co-producer Phoebe Wang, there were times when the team found the project challenging. 'At times I felt as though I'd throw my hands up in the air and say "I honestly don't think I can do this anymore!"' said Phoebe, 'but these circumstances made me really step up to make professional decisions as a producer.'

The hard work was ultimately rewarding for all those involved. Co-producer Katrina Gunara commented that the project required a lot of patience, passion and determination, but was also very fulfilling: 'Seeing and hearing the audience roar, and getting positive, excited responses after the show made the efforts put in truly worth it.' Her co-producer Phoebe shared similar sentiments: 'No amount of challenges could outweigh the immeasurable feeling of personal achievement and satisfaction I got from producing this show. This position has not only helped me develop as a leader, choreographer and dancer, but has also given me the opportunity to mature as a person.'

Figure 6.6   Students performing in Reverie at United World College, Singapore.

6

Now let's look at how Creativity can be used in to provide a Service for a migrant school in China.

CAS SNAPSHOT

Peer-mentoring project in China

A group of students at the British International School Shanghai (BISS), Puxi Campus, initiated a peer-mentoring system in a local migrant school in Shanghai. The CAS project aimed to foster leadership, empowerment and cross-cultural understanding between children in the migrant school system and the international school system in Shanghai. Students were able to interact one-to-one with migrant children to help run the daily programme and establish meaningful connections with their migrant 'buddy'. After being involved in the programme, a group of students identified the need for an extra-curricular activities (ECA) club for the migrant school students. They investigated the needs and necessary resources to do this, and applied for a learning service grant. They were awarded 1 500 USD to start this project.

The following year the students raised awareness of this programme within the whole school and led ECA at the migrant school. The project involved 35 students in planning and leading activities including Arts and Crafts, Music, Science club, Eco club and Drama for the migrant school students. The students were able to lead younger students in planning sessions and delivering the ECA in the migrant school. The connection made between the schools has led to other new projects – BISS students are planning a film project where the local migrant schoolchildren will be taught how to use a camera and then given a camera to produce films about their own lives under the guidance of BISS film students.

Can you see any advantages of working in CAS projects that are based on more than one strand of CAS?

Is there a particular strand of CAS that you might find more interesting to base your CAS project on?

6.07 Review of Chapter 6

1 What are the key elements of a CAS project?

2 Are the CAS stages more important for CAS projects than for CAS experiences?

3 What current interests do you have that you could turn into ideas for a CAS project?

4 Explain the difference between a CAS project and a CAS experience.

5 In what ways do you see the attributes of the IB learner profile manifested in CAS projects?

6.08 A summary of this chapter

In this chapter we have:

- Described what will be expected of you when working on a CAS project
- Explored the nature of the CAS project
- Outlined how the CAS stages can be implemented in CAS projects
- Looked at CAS projects based on each of the three CAS strands, and projects that involve more than one strand
- Seen a number of different examples of CAS projects from different parts of the IB regions.

The CAS portfolio and student responsibilities

'Opportunity is missed by most people because it is dressed in overalls and looks like work.'

Thomas A. Edison

CAS provides a unique opportunity for you. It is the only area of your school where you can have total control. The choice is yours as to what experiences you undertake as part of your CAS programme. As such you have a great deal of freedom, but as always, freedom comes with responsibility.

The most important thing to have when approaching CAS is a positive and determined attitude. You need to take the initiative and take responsibility for yourself. The very fact that you are reading this shows that you care about your education and your CAS programme, so you are already on the right track. Well done, now read on!

The purpose of this chapter is to offer advice on creating a rewarding and enjoyable CAS. By the end of the chapter you should fully understand your responsibilities, and know how to organise your time and avoid common pitfalls. Following this advice will make your life much easier and take the pressure off your IB CAS programme.

7.01 An outline and explanation of student responsibilities

There is a great deal of detailed information throughout this book on what CAS is and how to make it work for you. Figure 7.1 provides a brief summary.

7

Figure 7.1 Summary of CAS.

Understanding

When embarking on your CAS programme, you need to understand the following points:

What CAS is about and for (see Chapter 1)

CAS is designed to make you a more rounded and balanced person. You may be a great scholar and be able to get top marks in all of your academic subjects, but if your only life experience is inside a library then you won't be a rounded and interesting individual. CAS is your chance to gain credit for all the other things you do in your life, or to give you the push to do different and interesting things that you always wanted to do. At the same time it can help you develop the attributes of the learner profile and other important life skills.

CAS requirements (see Chapter 2)

To complete the CAS programme you must be involved in a number of experiences, and at least one project, over a period of at least 18 months. These experiences should incorporate the three CAS strands.

CAS learning outcomes (LO)

The seven CAS learning outcomes are:

LO1. Identify your own strengths and develop areas for growth.

LO2. Demonstrate that challenges have been undertaken, developing new skills in the process.

LO3. Demonstrate how to initiate and plan a CAS experience.

LO4. Show commitment and perseverance in CAS experiences.

LO5. Demonstrate the skills and recognize the benefits of working collaboratively.

LO6. Demonstrate engagement with issues of global significance.

LO7. Recognize and consider the ethics of choices and actions.

CAS Guide (2015)

In your 18 months on the CAS programme you must show each LO at least once, although you may well demonstrate one or more of them many times!

The CAS stages (Chapter 2)

As highlighted in Chapter 2, the CAS stages are Investigation, Preparation, Action, Reflection and Demonstration. You should use the stage framework to plan for the majority of your CAS experiences. The amount of time and effort you spend on each stage will vary depending on the experience.

Plan and investigate

You need to plan a series of CAS experiences and a CAS project. Chapter 1 contains suggestions for how to undertake a proposal for a CAS activity, and Chapter 3 explains how to use the CAS framework for more in-depth experiences. Remember that you may already have experience of activities that you could use as part of your CAS programme, or some that may fit with a little adaptation.

7

Communication

You need to communicate regularly with your CAS Advisor or Coordinator. Keep in touch throughout your programme so that they can support you in staying on track. In addition, there are three specific meetings (see section 7.07), in which you will need to explain:

- Your plans for your CAS experiences and why they are suitable CAS experiences
- What LOs you have progressed towards during those experiences
- How you have reflected on your experiences
- How you will demonstrate your achievements.

Many schools use an electronic or online system for this communication, while others use paper-based methods. Whatever the method, use it regularly and often. Remember that your CAS Advisor is trying to help you to be successful in CAS. In many ways they are also your CAS examiner. So make their life easier and you will be rewarded by a supportive friend.

Reflection

As covered in earlier chapters (and particularly Chapter 3), reflecting on your CAS programme should help you to understand the impact of your experiences on you and the learning you have gained from them. It may also help you develop in other areas of your life, like your academic studies. This is a continuous process so make some time and space for purposeful reflection in your life.

Key point: Reflection is what helps us learn and make sense of our experiences.

Demonstration

You have to demonstrate what you have achieved in your CAS experiences by putting together a CAS portfolio. A sensible approach is to put this together as you go along so that you have a record of all of your CAS experiences.

CAS portfolio: 'A CAS Portfolio is used by students to plan their CAS programme, reflect on their CAS experiences and gather evidence of involvement in CAS'.

CAS Guide (2015), page 30

7.02 First steps – planning or preparation

To put together a successful CAS programme you need a variety of activities. It is up to you and your school to decide how many activities exactly; remember that this is your programme so you need to take responsibility for it.

Completing the following activity will help you to see the many and varied opportunities for CAS which exist in your community, and identify experiences you already undertake that could contribute to your CAS programme. This could be included as part of your CAS personal profile in your CAS portfolio.

> **CAS personal profile:** this is a summary of your interests, skills, talents and areas that you would like to develop. It can help you to think about your CAS programme as a coherent activity that fits together, perhaps with your career or university goals.

You do not necessarily need to stop your current activities outside of your academic studies to take up something else. You may need to adapt it slightly, but if you want to continue with an activity, you can work out a way, with your CAS Advisor, of continuing it and counting it as a CAS experiences. Fill in the first column of Table 7.1 to list the things you already do. Some may be obvious, such as playing in a school soccer team or an orchestra. You should even record activities that do not seem like potential CAS experiences, such as taking my sister to the park every Sunday, visiting my grandmother in the old people's home every month, playing on Playstation, watching Bollywood films.

You may have other things that you have always wanted to do or try. Now is your chance to find a way to undertake them as part of your CAS programme. Whatever is your heart's desire record it in the middle column of Table 7.1. It may be knitting a jumper, travelling to Nepal, taking part in a parachute jump or something that may help you prepare or decide on a future career or area of study.

Your school may already offer a choice of activities that you can participate in. This may be something that you can undertake with a support structure already in place. Even if your school does not offer clubs, teams or activities there are probably organisations in your town that do so. Find out about anything that is already happening in your school or town and fill in the third column of Table 7.1; there may be far more than you ever realised.

CAS experience: an event that you will count as part of your CAS. It may be a series of events, such as training and being in a team, or practising and then taking part in a performance, or it may be a one-off event such as marshalling a sports event, or a weekend mountain-biking.

CAS project: a special type of CAS experience; see Chapter 5.

CAS programme: a number of combined experiences that you undertake throughout your time studying the IB Diploma Programme. Some are large, in-depth experiences combining many events, while others are smaller, one-off events. Some programmes have many experiences, some have few.

Figure 7.2 A CAS programme consists of many CAS experiences, one of which is a CAS project.

ACTIVITY BOX

Experiences you already have outside of schoolwork	Experiences you are interested in pursuing	Experiences offered by your school or community

Table 7.1 Brainstorming CAS experiences.

Some activities may fit into all three of the columns.

Once you have undertaken this exercise you should have a good idea of the experiences you want to have during your CAS programme. Remember that you don't have to do everything at once, all the time. You can spread out your experiences throughout the 18 months, including the holidays.

However, just because you have found something that you want to undertake as a CAS experience, this does not mean that you can use it as a valid CAS experience. There is no list of what is and what is not a CAS experience. It is your job to convince the person in your school that what you plan to do is a valid CAS experience. They may ask you some awkward questions, so if you are prepared and able to answer these questions then you can use these to communicate your plans to your CAS teacher.

Key point: Look back at Chapter 1 for ideas for more strategies, including how to propose a new CAS experience and how to convert an existing experience into a CAS experience.

7

7.03 The CAS experience: your responsibilities

> **Key point:** What is valid CAS? The decision is up to your school CAS Coordinator. Just because another school accepts it does not mean that your school will, so communicate your plans early.

For each experience you plan to undertake, you must communicate with your school's CAS staff, who must agree that it is a valid experience. Communication is important as you would be very disappointed if you put a great deal of time and effort into an experience which is not accepted as valid CAS by your school.

If an adult is supervising your experience, make sure that they know you are undertaking this as a CAS experience. Some schools require forms to be signed by an adult supervisor for each experience. You may need to find a suitable time to explain to an adult what CAS is and what you are trying to achieve. The beginning of band practice or a nursing shift may not be the ideal time for that, so always make a suitable appointment. Prepare what you need to explain, and ask for help from your school if you think you need it.

> **Key point:** CAS supervisors are adults that offer guidance during the students' CAS experience (*CAS Guide* (2015)). They generally help students to get the most out of an experience and can be coaches, charity workers or other teachers with an interest in the experience. It is not always necessary to have a CAS supervisor, but many schools require them. Some schools also require that CAS supervisors provide feedback, written or otherwise, to a school as part of the experience. This can be included in a CAS portfolio.

For the majority of your CAS experiences using the CAS stages framework should be a great deal of help. You must then undertake the experience. This may seem pretty obvious, but sometimes you plan things that don't happen. Then you must reflect on the experience.

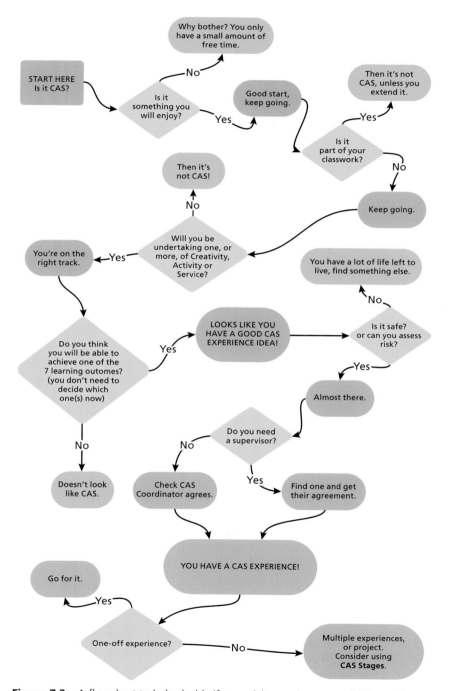

Figure 7.3 A flowchart to help decide if an activity can become a CAS experience.

7

Completing one of your CAS experiences

Once you have finished a CAS experience, you need to complete the process through reflection and demonstration, and communicate that you have done so to the CAS supervisor, your CAS Advisor or whatever supervisory method your school uses.

Don't forget this part of the experience: remember to make yourself easy to supervise and show that you are completing your CAS requirements. Many supervisors give up their time as volunteers so this is a good time to thank them for their help.

If you are continuing an activity after the end of your CAS programme, as many students do, then just choose an imaginary finishing point and inform your supervisors and school staff.

7.04 The CAS project: your responsibilities

You must be involved in at least one CAS project during your CAS programme.

As for all your CAS experiences you are expected to reflect on your CAS project(s). This is a good opportunity to have a group reflection with others that you have worked with on a project to understand other people's perceptions.

ACTIVITY BOX

Do an internet search for 'De Bono's six thinking hats' or 'Belbin's team roles'.

Consider your role in the CAS project and the roles that other participants undertook. Do any of these match a 'hat' or a team role? Fill in Tables 7.2 and 7.3 below.

This makes an ideal group reflection activity where each member of the group assigns a team role, or hat, to each member of the team and to themselves. They then explain why they have done so. Perhaps individuals wore different hats at different occasions, or performed different team roles. Expand this activity by considering other times when you may have to wear different hats or perform different roles. Perhaps in your next group project, or in your lab experiments?

Table 7.2 Belbin's team roles

Team role	Participant	Reason
Plant		
Resource instigator		
Coordinator		
Shaper		
Monitor evaluator		
Team worker		
Implementer		
Completer or finisher		
Specialist		

Table 7.3 De Bono's hats

Hat colour	Description	Participant	Reason
Blue	Process		
White	Objective		
Yellow	Positive		
Green	Creative		
Black	Negative		
Red	Intuitive		

As for all experiences, a CAS project uses one or more of the CAS strands (Creativity, Activity or Service) and you will likely meet one, or several, of the CAS learning outcomes.

Key point: There is more detailed information on CAS projects in Chapter 6, including how to develop a project out of a CAS experience you have already undertaken and examples of the different CAS projects in the three CAS strands.

7.05 Completing your entire CAS programme

Your school will set a deadline for completing your CAS requirements. This should be a minimum of 18 months after you have started your CAS programme. Be aware of this deadline and create a schedule leading up to it in which you follow the steps in 7.03 above. Build in enough time for feedback.

See Table 7.4: check that you have completed all seven of the learning outcomes and demonstrated that you have done so. If you are missing any, brainstorm how you might have actually achieved it in one of your experiences without demonstrating it. If you are concerned, communicate with your school CAS staff and reach a solution with them.

As the deadline approaches, take time to complete and review your CAS portfolio. Inform your CAS Coordinator when you are finished. You are likely to have one CAS interview left to review your portfolio. Look at section 7.07 below for advice on preparing for that.

Provide evidence of	✔	Date	Note
Planning a CAS programme			
CAS programme lasting 18 months with regular activity			
Creativity, Activity and Service included			
CAS Stages used when appropriate			
Minimum of one CAS project			
LO1: Identified strengths and areas for growth			
LO2: Undertaking new challenges and developing new skills			
LO3: Initiated and planned experience			
LO4: Commitment and perseverance			
LO5: Working collaboratively			
LO6: Engaged with issues of global importance			
LO7: Recognized and considered ethics of choices and actions			
Reflection happened when appropriate			
Supervisor feedback if needed			
CAS interviews 1, 2 and 3 completed			

Table 7.4   A checklist for completing your CAS programme.

All of this evidence should be visible in your final CAS portfolio.

7.06 A suggested code of ethics in dealing with Service

Ethics are defined as the moral principles that govern a person's behaviour or the conducting of an activity (in this case, a CAS experience or project). See Chapter 5 for in-depth information on CAS and ethics.

The seventh CAS LO concerns ethics. CAS Service experiences deal with ethics in the decision-making process. Ethics may be considered doing the right thing, but also doing something for the right reasons.

Key point: Ethics is also a topic in the TOK course. Your TOK teacher may be able to help you with these questions, or you may be able to find more information in TOK resources in the library.

If you are providing a service for someone or something then you are entering an ethical dimension even if you do not realise it. You must ask yourself some very important ethical questions including:

- Why am I doing this?
- What do I want to achieve?
- Have I asked the people affected by my Service about their opinions?
- Can I keep my promises?

In addition you may wish to develop a code of practice for your project. The following activity will help you consider the ethics of your experience in more detail and bring ethical awareness to your CAS programme.

ACTIVITY BOX

Draw up a list of questions your need to ask before you begin a Service activity.

Does your school have an ethical code for CAS experiences? Could you write one? Perhaps you could undertake this activity within a TOK class. Here are some starting points:

1 Experiences/projects must respect the rights, interests and dignity of participants and related persons in the project.

2 Experiences/projects must be undertaken in accordance with any relevant law.

3 Freely informed consent should normally be obtained from participants.

4 The design of an experience and its conduct should ensure integrity.

What would you add or take away?

Many of the students studying an IB Diploma Programme are very lucky to have a high standard of food, shelter and education. However, it is vital to understand that being in this privileged position does not mean that you have all of the answers to life's problems, and in any case money is not always the solution. Groups we aim to serve must be treated with the utmost respect and consideration.

Key point: Want to know more about the different types of Service? Read Chapter 4.

7.07 Activities to prepare for the mandatory CAS interviews

CAS interviews should take place on three occasions during your CAS programme. They take place with a member of staff from your school who has responsibility for your CAS programme, such as the CAS Coordinator, a CAS Advisor, a homeroom teacher or a tutor.

The first interview happens at the beginning of your CAS programme. This to check that you understand what CAS is all about, including the requirements and learning outcomes, and to discuss your planned experiences and how you will demonstrate your CAS achievements.

The second interview is to check your progress in CAS towards the LOs, to see if you have a balanced programme and to offer advice and feedback on your Reflection and Demonstration. It happens partway through your CAS programme.

The third interview is generally done at the completion of your CAS programme. This interview should help you to reflect on your CAS programme, what you have enjoyed, how you have developed and how this experience may influence you in the future.

Use the following reminders to help you prepare for your CAS interviews at the various points in your CAS programme. These interviews should be enjoyable experiences to confirm that you are on the correct track to success. Below are some possible questions you may be asked, but the interviews depend on your experiences and how well you have communicated with your CAS staff member.

ACTIVITY BOX

Preparing for the first CAS interview

- Read this chapter!
- Complete the first activity in this chapter or create a CAS personal profile.
- Select some CAS experiences that you plan to do.
- Sample interview questions

1 Do you have any questions about CAS?
2 What are you excited about? What is challenging?
3 How will CAS enable you to grow? Is that connected to the learner profile?
4 How will you plan a CAS programme that includes Creativity, Activity and Service?
5 How will you manage your time to include CAS in your Diploma Programme?
6 What does your personal profile look like?
7 What experiences are you planning to undertake?
8 Is there anything you need help with?
9 Do you understand the CAS learning outcomes? Which do you think is challenging?

10 Do you have a method for demonstrating your CAS achievements, evidence and reflection?

Adapted from *CAS Teacher Support Material* (2015) IBO

ACTIVITY BOX

Preparing for the second CAS interview

- Complete all the experiences, using the guidance in this chapter.
- Update your portfolio fully to demonstrate your achievements.
- Think about what connections you can make between your CAS experiences, between the CAS experiences and academic work, and between CAS experience and the rest of your life.

Sample interview questions

1 What have you achieved in your CAS experiences?
2 Which learning outcomes have you met or made progress in?
3 How has Reflection helped you in CAS?
4 Have you had ongoing participation in CAS experiences?
5 What has been most enjoyable/challenging/frustrating in your CAS experiences?
6 How have you used the CAS stages framework?
7 What development, personal or skills, have you made in a CAS project?
8 What have you learnt from CAS?
9 Have you been able to connect your experience in CAS to academic subjects or other areas of your life?
10 Have you undertaken Creativity, Activity and Service?

Adapted from *CAS Teacher Support Material* (2015) IBO

ACTIVITY BOX

Preparing for the third CAS interview

- Finalise all of your CAS experiences.
- Complete your portfolio, including Reflection and Demonstration.

- Think about how your CAS experiences have changed you, what you have learnt and how you can apply this in the future.

Sample interview questions

1 What did you enjoy most/least about your CAS programme?
2 Did you overcome a challenge that you are proud of?
3 What have you achieved through CAS?
4 What will you take from these experiences?
5 Describe your role in the CAS project(s); did you always have the same role?
6 What role has Reflection had in your CAS experiences?
7 How did the learning outcomes help you to develop as a person? Which one made the most impact on you?
8 How could CAS be improved in our school?

Adapted from *CAS Teacher Support Material* (2015) IBO

7.08 The structure of the CAS portfolio

Like many aspects of the IB Diploma Programme, it is imperative that to make your life easier you are organised from the very beginning of your Diploma.

Whichever method you choose, or your school uses, for creating a CAS portfolio, start creating it as soon as you begin your CAS programme. Record your evidence, categorise it by experiences, and keep an overview of different aspects completed. Remembering that you could easily complete each learning outcome more than once, but you must complete each outcome at least once.

7

Methods of recording CAS 1; paper file, developmental workbook or scrapbook

Believe it or not, CAS existed before computers were ubiquitous, and we all coped perfectly well! If you choose to use a paper method of evidencing your CAS, follow these steps:

1 Buy a large file, plastic wallets and file dividers.

2 Keep track of which learning outcomes and requirements you have completed (you could use the checklist Table 7.4 earlier in this chapter), and make a contents page.

3 Include your CAS personal profile, or the first activity in this chapter, if you have completed either of these.

4 Create a section for each of your experiences. In each section include:
   • Investigation, planning or proposal
   • Evidence of completing the activity, such as photos, tickets or anything else useful
   • Completed reflection activities
   • Supervisor feedback if necessary.

5 Consider having a section to record your interviews and overall thoughts on your CAS programme, not just your individual CAS experiences.

In order for your CAS portfolio to be monitored, you will need to bring it into school to allow the member of staff to look at it.

The scrapbook method is great for people who like to write, draw and include their reflections and evidence in this way. You can also keep and annotate other evidence such as tickets, souvenirs and photographs in this file. However, if you record a film, audio or other digital media, you can only place a link to this in the file.

When you have finished your scrapbook you can keep it as a memento of your CAS programme and the many memories it generated.

Key point: University and job applications are now increasingly competitive. Universities and employers want more from people than good qualifications or grades. CAS is a way of showing that you are a rounded, balanced person who has interests outside academic work, who can fit into a team and work well with a new group. Keep your CAS portfolio and use it to help write applications in the future.

Methods of recording CAS 2: ICT

Key point: There are several commercial and non-commercial options available for recording your CAS experiences.

ManageBac, myCAS and Gibbon have specific options for students to record their CAS experiences and reflections online, and keep track of completed learning outcomes. It is also possible to use a collaborative cloud service to share and organise your CAS reflections and evidence such as Moodle, Dropbox, Edmodo or Google Classroom or Drive. Whichever system your school uses, you will quickly need to become familiar with it.

Figure 7.4 ManageBac

Figure 7.5 Gibbon

Whichever ICT or web-based solution you use to create a CAS portfolio, it is imperative that you realise that the system does not do the whole job for you.

Although the webpage may give you a space to record reflection, it does not ask pertinent questions and it does not know what you have been through. It is still up to you to take responsibility for considering your experiences, recording them and taking time out for meaningful reflection.

Key point: Struggling with Reflection? Check out Chapter 3 for lots of advice and ideas on ways and methods to reflect.

Some commercial programs keep everything well-organised in a space that is available to you, your supervisor, advisor and CAS Coordinator. This means that everyone can easily monitor what you are doing in real time. You will however have to complete your reflection and upload other forms of evidence.

If you are using a cloud service like Dropbox or Google Drive, you can follow the advice for paper file above, the only difference being that you do not need to bring it to school to have it checked; you just share it with your supervisor.

Links are easily added to YouTube videos, blogs or other websites that you may have used or created in your portfolio. However, if you have other souvenirs or non-digital work, you may need to take photographs and add these instead.

Table 7.5 considers the advantages and disadvantages of using digital and paper files.

Paper		Computer or web-based	
Advantages	Disadvantages	Advantages	Disadvantages
Good memento of CAS programme	Have to hand in to school to be checked	School staff can monitor your progress easily	Requires access to computer to complete
Cheap	Hard to record non-written methods in it	Can create links to video, photo, written, oral and other reflection	Can have cost implications
	If you lose it, you're in trouble!	Should be backed up	Still possible to lose everything!
Can record non-digital evidence (e.g. a play programme)		Could convert non-digital evidence using photography	Need to be digitally literate and have facilities available

Table 7.5 Advantages and disadvantages of paper and digital files.

7.09 The role of a student CAS committee

Several schools have an in-school Service option of joining or creating a CAS committee. If your school does not have one and you are interested in the role, then why not make a proposal to form one as one of your CAS experiences?

The role of the committee is to be responsible for communication about CAS to the school community and beyond. Examples of tasks may include setting up web pages or maintaining display boards. The committee may develop a CAS handbook for the use of the student body or guidance for non-school CAS supervisors, or support the CAS programme in other appropriate ways.

The CAS committee could undertake the majority of the research in the first activity in this chapter and find all the activities offered in the school and town. This would be a valuable resource for all the students in the Diploma Programme in your school, and would only need to be updated once a year.

7.10 Review of Chapter 7

1   What is the most important thing to have in CAS?

2   What are the learning outcomes?

3   What are, and when, should you use CAS stages?

4   How do you complete an experience?

5   What do you need to do to complete your entire CAS programme?

6   How many interviews should you have, and when do they occur?

7.11 A summary of this chapter

In this chapter we have considered:

* Your role as a student in your CAS programme
* What you need to understand to have a successful CAS programme
* How to begin planning a programme and reviewed what defines a CAS experience
* The logistics for an experience and a project
* How to complete an experience and your CAS programme
* The need to be organised, and looked at how to record your CAS portfolio, including the advantages and disadvantages of paper or ICT methods
* How to prepare for your three CAS interviews
* The idea of a CAS committee.

Celebration
of CAS

8

Creativity, Activity and Service is one of the most challenging and rewarding parts of the IB Diploma Programme, and as such you should take the opportunity to celebrate your achievements. It is not a question of being egotistic but rather recognising where you have travelled to as a person. This can also be a fitting climax to your school career.

In many cases CAS experiences happen unnoticed by other members of the school and local community, so celebrating them raises awareness of what you have done. Other students in the school will realise from your example that CAS offers a number of opportunities for personal growth and development. Sometimes this will mean that you have been responsible for engaging other students in a project; your enthusiasm for the work that you have done may be infectious!

Informing others of your CAS experiences may also lead them to build on your efforts and extend your work. This is especially relevant to experiences and projects involving Service. By being exposed to your service learning achievements, others may see opportunities to implement similar work in different contexts, or to continue the work you have done. We will see in this chapter examples of CAS experiences growing into larger projects, and the importance of celebrating CAS.

Public celebration of your CAS, both by you as an individual and also by your school, provides an opportunity to demonstrate the contributions of the school to the community. Knowledge of your school's CAS experiences may help to lift the profile of the school through the local newspaper or television channel and help to strengthen links with your local community.

In this chapter we shall be looking at some examples of celebrating CAS. There are a number of possibilities that we shall mention, including at school level: assemblies, web pages, newsletters, and your own YouTube channel and/or Facebook page. Of course you can also look at the possibility of organising and running a special CAS day.

8.01 Celebration of CAS in schools

School assemblies

One of the best ways of sharing information at your school is to organise an assembly about your CAS experiences or projects. You could ask for time at full school or grade-level assemblies to talk about your particular project. At the Intercommunity School in Zurich, one of the traditions of the school was that students were given a chance to talk to their peers about the CAS projects they had been involved with over the summer holidays. This was often one of the times when students could share their CAS experiences in public reflections. The students developed clear ideas of each others' projects, and there was a chance to recognise special achievements. Some examples included:

1   Cycling through Switzerland from east to west (which was undertaken over a week)

2   A dune re-vegetation programme in the German Island of Sylt

3   Collecting clothes for a Russian orphanage and then delivering them to the children

4   Working with disabled people in a sheltered workshop

5   Writing, directing and participating in a play.

Organising publicity for CAS through Facebook

One very effective way of publicising CAS within school is to have notices and information about your CAS project on a school Facebook page for CAS. The International School of Brussels has a very well-used and effective Facebook page. This has provided students with a tool for both reflecting on their CAS experiences and sharing information with each other and members of the school community. The school's Facebook page was the main vehicle for organising and celebrating a project to unite the school through poetry, project called 'Poems Through the Glass Walls'.

8

CAS SNAPSHOT

'"Poems Through the Glass Walls" was a large-scale CAS project based on the successful project in London called "Poems on the Underground", in which people either write or send in poems to be put up in and around the Underground in London where people walking everyday can see them.

'This project was created by students, for the student community. Its aim was to unite the International School of Brussels' student community by allowing all sections of the school (from the Early Childhood Center to the High School) to write a piece of poetry. After a selection process, the work was then put up onto ISB's "glass walls" with acetate paper, allowing the poems to be clearly seen *through* the glass walls. By having meetings and presentations about the project with the students, the teachers and the heads of the school divisions, the project was known throughout the student community. Other aspects such as the "Poems Through the Glass Walls" website, the publicity on the ISB website, the Facebook page, the anthology and the promotional video, really helped to publicise this project to the community. Once the poems were up, they could be seen everywhere, allowing the students from all the sections to admire and read the poetry.'

Thomas, International School of Brussels.

Figure 8.1 The CAS wall at Tonbridge Grammar School, UK.

Public displays of CAS in the school

Most schools have noticeboards which are used to advertise CAS experiences and display work. Figure 8.1 shows an example from Tonbridge Grammar School.

They can evolve into a place that can be used in a very creative way to help bring a school community together. This has great potential in a boarding school where people come from very different countries and cultures. The girls at Cheltenham Ladies' College in the UK had a brilliant idea of getting students and staff to bring a postcard of their homes and put them together in a huge collage.

CAS CASE STUDY

Celebrating community, diversity, global citizenship and interconnectedness

It's an old and perhaps corny adage, but to know where you're going, it's important to always remember where you've come from. At Cheltenham Ladies' College (CLC) the practical reality of this phrase is truly remarkable and fantastically exciting. With girls from dozens of cultures, countries and backgrounds living and learning together, CLC is a fascinating environment in which to learn.

The diversity of their community was brought to life by an innovative project focusing on where members of the school community come from. What started as an inspiring idea by a small group of students quickly blossomed into a piece of work that encompassed the whole school. The pupils recognised that among their peers and the school staff was an array of enriching and enlightening tales that needed to be told. They thought a vibrant and colourful display would be the best way to do this, so 1000 blank postcards were produced and distributed among the students and staff. Everybody took part, in writing on a postcard from home, from the youngest Year 7 student to long-serving members of grounds and maintenance staff, resulting in a colourful, inspiring, amusing and insightful display.

The postcards were combined to produce a banner 13 m long and 1.5 m high to display in a prominent location in College. Students, staff and visitors marvelled at the final piece for weeks. Visitors to the tapestry are asked to consider what binds the school community, what they value, how they can make the most of international links, whether it is possible to see beyond their personal perspective and think differently. Their responses formed the basis of a fascinating assembly.

Students tracked the whole project by using Instagram, created a 'making of' video, and produced a time-lapse video of people looking at the banner. With students coming from over 40 countries they learnt a lot about the world from each other. Overall, the 'Our Stories' project helped students to develop a sense of identity, interdependence and intercultural understanding as well as encouraging the whole school to engage in the process of reflection, sharing and listening.

This following reflection on the project is from Grace, a student at CLC.

'Being part of the "Our Stories" project has been a really good experience. It showed me the extent of the rich international and cultural diversity we have here at college, and how our countries of origin shape our perspectives that were displayed through the postcards. I think one of the highlights for me during the "Our Stories" project was collecting the postcards into a banner. I learnt so much while sorting the postcards out, not just about the individuals that comprise our community but about their countries as well, and some people had very interesting facts about themselves or about the world. Some of the best postcards to read were those from the school staff we do not normally have conservations with, and I think this project really showcased a different and unseen aspect of the college community. Working with the rest of the group, brainstorming about ideas and how we could continue carrying the project forward, was also always a great time and I liked having that Monday afternoon to talk and share the different ideas we had; this was one of the reasons why a group of us decided to start Global Citizens Society. I think the best part of the "Our Stories" project was definitely seeing the banner being hung up at school, and having that visual representation and appreciation of how our individual little stories put together formed a large cohesive body. I am glad that I was part of this process.'

Figure 8.2   Girls at Cheltenham Ladies' College making their display.

Could you celebrate the diversity in your school by organising something similar?

Promoting your CAS activities or projects in local newspapers

Local newspapers often carry a phone number or an email address so that members of the public can send details of newsworthy stories or events. Try contacting a newspaper with a news story about your CAS activities or projects – sending them a media release (see below) would be recommended. A reporter may then call you back for more information, or even visit your school. When you make initial contact, try to give as much information about the project as possible and why it will be interesting to their readers. If you have photographs to include then do so, or suggest a time that a reporter or photographer could visit to get details, interviews and photographs. To see your name in print and your activity celebrated is a great reward; it will also promote the activity to other people and promote the school in the local community.

Figure 8.3 Use the local press to publicise your CAS activities or projects.

SPOTLIGHT ON ... THE MEDIA RELEASE

This information supplied to the media – newspapers, magazines or online sites – is called a media release. The framework below could also be used within your school community for newsletters, bulletins, emails to parents or yearbooks.

Write your release following this template:

Headline
The headline of your release should summarise the key point of your CAS experience/project, using catchy and interesting language. Write a headline which attracts attention and encourages further reading.

Lead
The lead paragraph is very important. It acts as a hook to ensure that the audience reads on. It needs to outline your message directly and concisely, and should include: WHO will do/did it? WHAT will/did they do? WHERE will/did they do it? WHEN will/did they do it? WHY will/did they do it? HOW will/did they do it?

Body
The paragraph following the lead should add details to the points made in the lead paragraph. Expand on the who, what, where, and so on. Make sure you order the information from most to least important. Use short sentences and short paragraphs, writing in the third person and using interesting and engaging language! You might want to include a quote from one of the people involved in your CAS to add more interest.

End
End the release with a concise paragraph about your CAS experience/ project, and include details of who to contact for more information.

8.02 Another way of celebrating CAS – a TEDx conference

One of the ways of celebrating CAS and pursuing some of the themes which students are interested in is to organise a TEDx conference at your school. The International School of Kuala Lumpur organised one of these events, which drew on the many talents of the students who were in the school. In addition, they had to learn to comply with the regulations that are necessary to host a TED event.

TED: is an abbreviation of Technology, Education and Design. A TEDx event is a local gathering where live TED-like talks and videos previously recorded at TED conferences are shared with the community. TEDx events are fully planned and coordinated independently, on a community-by-community basis. The content and design of each TEDx event is unique and developed independently, but all of them have features in common.

www.ted.com/participate/organize-a-local-tedx-event/before-you-start/
what-is-a-tedx-event

CAS SNAPSHOT

TED Talks are known for their 'ideas worth spreading'. Rather than just viewing them on YouTube, wouldn't it be exciting to organise a TEDx event right at your own school? This is exactly what one IB Diploma Programme candidate decided to do as her CAS project: 'Since my old school hosted a TEDx conference, I kept thinking about holding one [here] as well. Finally, I decided it was time to take action and actually try to make it a reality!'

What followed was a series of meetings and work sessions involving some 40 students collaborating on different committees for about seven months. Their work began by getting the school's approval and obtaining a license from TED. Then the Curation Committee began searching for the kinds of people who would be able to ignite the 'Creative Spark', the event's theme. And the Events and Tech Committees were formed to facilitate the delivery of 12 inspiring speeches to an audience of about 300 young and seasoned adults.

The Curation Committee had to undertake the challenge of finding 12 dynamic and diverse speakers. Once the 12 speakers were finalised, communication about presentations meeting the TED regulations were provided. Sponsorships also had to be solicited. These required the committee members to 'take on a mature personality and professional manners' in their correspondences, reported another collaborator.

The event, with its regulations, was an opportunity for students to learn about social entrepreneurship and how challenging societal issues can give rise to creative solutions. It brought the school and outside communities together. The 'Creative Spark' was ignited in the hearts and minds of the organisers, audience and speakers alike.

Figure 8.4 Members of the Curation Committee from TEDx@ISKL.

Would you like to host a TEDx Conference in your school?

How would you go about it? (visit www.**ted**.com/participate/organize-a-local-**tedx-event)**

8.03 Celebrating CAS with your own project website

Many students have established projects that they want to continue for a long time. Setting up a website not only recognises and celebrates your efforts, it can also publicise your achievements to the world at large and help raise interest in your project. If the project involves fund-raising, this provides you with the opportunity to explain why the project is worthy of support and persuading potential sponsors that they should be helping you to achieve your project's aims. Jehona Gutaj, Ella Liskens and Sarah McCowan, students at the International School of Zug and Luzern, set up the website http://helpingthemotherteresasociety.weebly.com/ to support their project which was to raise money for a charity in Kosovo. Figure 8.5 is a screenshot from their website.

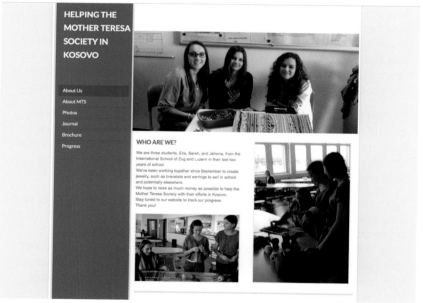

Figure 8.5 Helping the Mother Teresa Society.

Key point: Social media and other online tools are a great way of letting people know about your CAS involvement.

CAS CASE STUDY

Jehona's motivation for establishing this project and website

'I started making jewellery for my personal project in 10th grade, then I decided to sell it in school and donate the money to Kosovo. When I was researching which organisation I could donate it to, the Mother Teresa Association was the only one that seemed to exist. I asked my grandfather and family living in Kosovo to visit the office to make sure it really did exist and the money would go where I wanted it to go to. In that school year I donated 600 CHF to around 10 families in Kosovo.

'In 11th grade (1st year of IB) one of my friends (Ella) asked me if I wanted to keep the project going for our CAS project. We started making bracelets in our free time, and planned dates to sell them. While we were making bracelets another friend (Sarah) wanted to join us, and this is how we started our CAS project. Each one of us made bracelets at home, and every Thursday during lunchtime we sold the bracelets to students in our school. This went very well: we enjoyed making the bracelets and working together, and it was also nice for me to arouse the interest of other students who did not know much about the country itself. This project was especially important for me because going back to Kosovo to visit my family every year and seeing so many people struggle everyday made me want to help. The CAS project was a chance for me to start helping out.

'During the project we realised that the bracelets were not as popular as time passed, as almost everyone from our school had already bought them, so we started selling baked goods as well as the bracelets at other schools. The bracelets were still our main focus but we expanded our products in order to reach our goal which was to raise 1000 CHF.

'Once we had collected 1000 CHF, I went to Kosovo to visit the organisation. Throughout this day I was able to go with the volunteers from the organisation to a shopping centre where bags with essential goods (e.g. flour, cleaning products, bread, pasta, salt, and so on) were already packed for us to pick up. After this we went to visit families where we delivered the bags. I was able to visit an apartment building where most of the families that the money went to, lived. Being able to be there and experience the money really being used to help the families made me proud of my friends, myself and everyone who had donated. It was one of the most touching moments in my life, and I wanted to keep helping. This is how I started asking more friends to help out, and ended up inspiring a friend from my Swiss school to go and spend four months working with the association. I am also planning to extend this project and start something with Albanian students from my university to keep helping the families in need.

'We recorded our achievements on our website and at the end of the project made a presentation to our school. This gave us the chance to show what we had achieved and make sure the students who purchased the bracelets knew where their money had been spent.'

Jehona Gutaj, International School of Zug and Luzern, Switzerland.

This really emphasises the celebration of a successful CAS project and of a determined individual to help people in her homeland.

Another project that embraced the idea of creating a website both to promote and celebrate a CAS activity was 'Save the Perros' from a school in Chile. A problem that existed in Santiago was the prevalence of wild dogs in the streets. They wished to raise awareness about it and help to improve the welfare of the dogs. Below are some excerpts from their experiences of some of the problems they faced in setting up their website.

CAS SNAPSHOT

'Our project was to create a website to raise awareness about the issue of stray dogs in Santiago, Chile. This website's aim was to collect donations to support organisations involved in the welfare and sterilisation of the dogs.

'Our current website was launched in February 2015 after a number of problems that we experienced with our previous efforts. We spent a substantial amount of time working on the content (pictures, videos and textual information) as well as designing it to be easily accessible and visually pleasing. In addition to this, we created a YouTube account dedicated to the club's videos; linked the website to the Facebook group so that it would be easier to find; and uploaded pictures to show some of the dogs we have worked with and what our club does.

'A number of technical issues arose in connection to the design of our website. We resolved the problems by making changes to the platform and adding security. For example: the website was hard to edit as not everyone could work with HTML. After some reflection, we made the editing process more user-friendly so that all members could edit and post on the website.

'A couple of key things that we learnt in designing this project were the importance of collaboration and how much we relied on the talents of many different people in the group. The project also required our perseverance and commitment to the task.'

Save the Perros Project, International School Nido de Aguilas, Santiago, Chile.

8

8.04 CAS fairs – another celebration

In Ecuador and other Latin American countries, as well as across schools in Hong Kong, an innovative way of celebrating CAS has been for students to organise a CAS fair. Students have set up stalls within their schools with details about their CAS projects. Members of the local community are invited to join in the fair, as are students from local schools. This has been a great success as the wider community have learnt what the students are doing to contribute to their wellbeing.

Key point: CAS fairs are a great way for the local community to understand the involvement of students at an IB school in the general functioning of their community.

8.05 Celebrations of CAS with other schools

In Latin America and Europe there have been a number of joint celebrations of CAS, often focused around a certain theme. For example, in Ecuador there was a National InterCAS in 2014 that brought together students and their coordinators from over 20 schools. This kind of event provides a chance to learn about a particular theme for CAS, to carry out some joint Service experiences and to share CAS achievements together. It is a wonderful experience for all involved and brings out the joy of doing CAS. The InterCAS in 2014 had the following theme:

The purpose of the project was to develop a sense of awareness of autism in the Ecuadorian society. We engaged in this project by using our initiative and knowledge of dogs to provide therapy to people with autism. The aims of the project are to motivate students and society in general, to integrate people with autism into society and to learn about this condition of life.

> **InterCAS:** a conference of CAS students and coordinators that is held in Latin America on an annual basis. Students work together on a service project and have the chance to reflect and share experiences. They have been held in Mexico, Ecuador and Colombia.

CAS SNAPSHOT

InterCAS in Europe

The InterCAS concept has not been confined to the Americas but has also occurred in Europe, the Middle East and in the Asia/Pacific region. The KOC school in Turkey has organised two such events, inviting schools from the Middle East and Europe to attend. In 2011 the KOC school in conjunction with the Sanko School in Gaziantep hosted a conference which was focused on the history and creation of mosaics. This InterCAS focused on the CAS strand of Creativity, giving students the chance to visit museums in the city and then create mosaics themselves. This proved to be a really challenging task, and students were full of admiration for the ancient craftsman that created the wonderful mosaics in the museums. The students from IB schools in Turkey, Lebanon and the UK had the chance to mix with each other and work together to share CAS experiences (there were presentations by each of the participating schools on their CAS projects). Included in the programme were reflection through drama, and examining how the skills learnt in TOK could facilitate reflection better.

InterCAS experiences can help to establish the sense of international mindedness that the IB promotes.

8

8.06 Celebrating your CAS achievements in personal statements and university applications

Universities in the US, Britain and increasingly in other countries are looking to recruit students to their universities who are not just good students, but who are also going to contribute positively to the university community. They want students who are trying to make the world a better place to live in, and will enhance the reputation of the university in a cultural field or sport. A former Diploma Programme student who now attends Harvard College in the US said:

'All the students I met were smart. That was a first for my educational experience. Not only were they smart, but they had done amazing things, e.g. working in soup kitchens, performing on stage in public or representing their country in sport.'

It is amazing to see the number of IB students who forget at interviews or in their personal statements to universities to celebrate their own achievements in CAS, the extended essay or TOK. The core of the IB Diploma Programme sets you apart from other students who may have pursued a very narrow, academic, national matriculation course.

Why not make a short list of things you have done for CAS to help you write this personal statement or prepare you for university?

8.07 Review of Chapter 8

1 Why is it important to celebrate CAS?

2 List some of the ways in which you can celebrate CAS in school.

3 How can a CAS experience help to bring a school community together?

4 What benefits do you see from creating a CAS website to celebrate and promote your CAS project?

5 Why do you think it is important to organise a CAS experience with a number of other schools?

6 How can you use your CAS experiences to help your university applications?

8.08 A summary of this chapter

- There are many ways to celebrate CAS within the school such as at assemblies, CAS displays and on social media networks.
- Students have discovered effective ways of celebrating their achievements through webpages, YouTube and other online tools.
- You can also celebrate CAS through local newspapers.
- InterCAS conferences and workshops can be important communal ways for students from different schools to celebrate CAS together.
- Your CAS achievements can be very useful when writing university applications.

CAS and the approaches to learning

The approaches to learning (ATL) are part of a broad educational approach to prepare you for life after school. They are part of all IB programmes, and have most recently been introduced into the Diploma Programme. This chapter will focus on how the five categories of ATL skills used by the IB apply to your CAS programme. We shall start with a brief outline of the categories that the IB use for their ATL skills, and look at some of the issues raised by each. We will then explore each of the skills in more detail, providing examples of how these can be relied upon or developed in CAS, and challenge you to discover how you could utilise and enhance these skills through your CAS participation.

9.01 Approaches to learning (ATL) skills

The five categories that the IB has defined as ATL skills are:

1 Thinking skills (see section 9.01):
  This involves analysing and evaluating issues and ideas. Many of the issues here are ones that you deal with regularly, such as proposing and evaluating a range of solutions to problems and evaluating risk. In addition, it means generating new ideas and considering new perspectives. (An important part of this could be coming with an original solution to a problem.) A third significant area is being able to apply skills and knowledge to different situations.

2 Communication skills (see section 9.02):
  This means focusing on your ability to exchange ideas and thoughts with other people in a variety of ways (verbally, in writing, digitally). This is also vitally important in CAS, for example when collaborating with other students to prepare a project.

3 Social skills (see section 9.03):
  The key social skill is being able to work collaboratively and effectively with others. This is an essential core ability that you need for successful CAS experiences, and especially in the CAS project.

4 Self-management (see section 9.04):
  These are skills that are important for organising your CAS experiences around the rest of your life. Probably one of the most

9

difficult issues at the start of the Diploma Programme is time management. Other issues here are managing your approach to CAS (e.g. showing perseverance and commitment, maintaining motivation and being resilient after setbacks).

5   Research skills (see section 9.05):
This involves being able to find, analyse and interpret information. This can be very important to CAS when you are trying to prepare for a Service experience or develop a CAS project. Research may actually form the basis of a CAS experience in Service.

Each of these ATL skill sets are important in developing a balanced and meaningful CAS programme.

The following section gives examples of the ATL skills in CAS.

Thinking skills

Key point: In Chapters 2 and 3 we have looked at some of the key thinking skills that we use during CAS experiences. For the CAS stage of Investigation, when we investigate a particular type of experience we are combining research skills with the ability to *analyse* and *interpret* information that we have received from the individual or the community. The account below is an example of input from the people affected by the project helping students to analyse and rethink what they were doing.

CAS SNAPSHOT

A group of students were working with an asylum seekers' centre in Zurich. Many of the asylum seekers had come from African states and had very little clothing. The students launched a campaign to collect clothes for them. Most of the clothes collected were summer clothes (t-shirts, shorts, polo shirts, light trousers, summer dresses and cotton pullovers), but these were inappropriate for the coming winter. The asylum seekers politely made the point that while they were glad of the clothes, they really could do with winter clothes. The students then had to rethink their appeal and collection of clothes so that they focused on getting winter clothing. They had an overwhelming response, with good ski jackets and winter coats being donated in large numbers. This helped to provide the asylum seekers with appropriate clothing for winter.

Critical thinking skills

Two of the most significant critical thinking skills that are used in CAS experiences are reflective thinking, and the ability to identify obstacles and develop ways of overcoming them. We shall discuss them in more detail below.

CAS SNAPSHOT

'A fellow student and I went to the Herbstfest (autumn festival) in the city hall of Gersthofen to assist a group of disabled people. In total between 600 and 800 disabled people attended the festival with their supervisors.

'The instructions I was given by the supervisor were very different to what I was expecting. I thought I would need to help with caring for the disabled people, for instance helping them to eat or pushing their wheelchair around. But my main purpose was really to entertain them.

'At first I was quite unsure about how to relate to them. But as I got used to talking to them, going with them around the event and dancing with them, it gave me a completely unexpected insight. They were very vibrant and independent, and demonstrated that they really appreciated having someone to talk to, who showed an interest in them. I think communicating with people other than their supervisors made them feel more part of the event.

'Furthermore, I found it so fascinating how much happiness they gained from this event. One disabled man who was sitting beside me could not stop repeating how much he liked the food, while pasta with tomato sauce would not be considered very extraordinary by most people. This positive attitude is something I will definitely keep in mind, as well as remembering how fortunate able-bodied people are not to be physically or mentally restricted. This doesn't mean those who are disabled are less happy; the people whom I met seemed happy and were very generous. This is something that I learnt from the day: to appreciate small things in life and treat everybody nicely, with respect.'

Diana, International School of Augsburg, Germany.

The skill of reflective thinking is emphasised in Chapter 3. This book also contains many different examples of reflective thinking from students from a wide range of different contexts.

Identification of obstacles and how to overcome them

This is one of the important thinking skills. You may remember in Chapter 8 on the celebration of CAS the example given of setting up a website to advertise and celebrate a CAS project that students were creating for dog welfare in Chile. One of the great challenges this group of students faced was learning how to get a website hosted and saved on a server. This proved to be very challenging for them, and they went through a period of trial and error to find a solution to the problem. Below are some comments about the process they followed:

CAS SNAPSHOT

'We had a meeting with the club advisor, to understand what she wanted to include in the website, and after the meeting we drew up an outline to follow for the website.

'We purchased the domain name in September 2014, and put up the first website in October. We then took our time to learn how to navigate and edit the website, since this was a new skill that we had to acquire ourselves. Unfortunately the server hosting all the data crashed, and as we had not saved the data, everything had vanished. As a result, we learnt from our mistakes and created a second website, which unfortunately was hacked; all the data was lost again. The current website is now hosted on Cpanel, and we changed the default ports for many of the services and acquired SSL as a form of reducing vulnerability. The website went live in February 2015, and is now functioning well. During this process we learnt how to increase security for our website and ensure that all of the hard work we had put into creating the data was not lost.'

ACTIVITY BOX

1 Can you think of a situation in CAS where you have been confronted with a problem that you have analysed and then found a solution for?

2 What strategies did you use to overcome this problem?

3 How did you generate ideas?

4 How did you apply skills and knowledge to different areas?

Evaluate and manage risks

An important aspect of all CAS experiences for you, is being aware of the social, environmental and physical risks involved in carrying out a CAS experience and thinking about how to manage them. This means thinking through the situation and what solutions you might have to carry out for a particular experience.

CAS SNAPSHOT

Elton was a student who decided that he wanted to work in a soup kitchen in London. He needed to contact the organisation and also to arrange accommodation in a hostel in London. This was his first visit to London, so he needed to ensure that he knew where he was going and also find out about the area where he would be staying. Elton organised some contact numbers in London, and obtained appropriate medical insurance. When he started working at the soup kitchen, the manager said that in the unlikely case of one of their clients becoming violent, he was to use a panic button.

Elton found that the best way to manage this potential risk was to be as friendly as possible to all of the clients. He also made sure that he knew where the first aid kit was, in case of mishaps in the kitchen, and also the nearest hospital.

Elton had a wonderful week working in the soup kitchen in London. He experienced no problems with the many and varied clients that he met there. It was one of the highlights of his CAS programme. Elton felt that he learnt a lot about life in a very short time, and found that the clients were very friendly and open with him. He also enjoyed being part of a large and enthusiastic team of helpers. However, he thought it had been a good idea to plan for the eventuality of an accident.

Figure 9.1 A soup kitchen with helpers distributing food to the clients of the kitchen.

There are other examples of risk management in Chapter 2 of this book.

Thinking creatively

So far in this section we have really only considered how we can use critical thinking skills in CAS. However, an important skill that you can develop further through your CAS experiences is an ability to think *creatively*.

CAS SNAPSHOT

Creativity in action at Colegio Gran Bretana, Bogotá Colombia

F. Alejandra Cháker, CAS Coordinator at Colegio Gran Bretana explains that the college looks for innovation, inquiry and curiosity in its pupils. The IB core subjects are combined with all three aspects of the CAS programme. For instance, English, Art and Technology are combined in a project called 'Screencast'; this provides a free online English lesson service to those who are starting to learn the language or for children who need help improving their language skills. The language project is also using Art and Technology as language, thus this project helps to improve students' skills and raise awareness on education as a global issue. Through the use of various visual languages, others benefit and experience learning in an unorthodox way. Thus, students as authors and creators of these language videos – which can be seen on YouTube – develop critical and creative thinking, and experience collaborative work during the construction and launch of every video.

Below is a student's reflection on this:

'In Screencast, we will create a show (a short YouTube video) that will serve as an introduction to English for people who have never learnt it before. My teammates and I will create the medium to present the video (puppets, animation, drawings, and so on), design a script, take on a role and record the story.

'This activity was outside my comfort zone, as it involved a lot of social interaction, a weakness of mine. However, I have grown in that area, from sharing my ideas to simply speaking well by voicing the character. It also felt nice to know that this video would be a gateway to people learning English, which gives many people opportunities. Overall, this activity was a good experience, and I have been affected for the better by participating in it.'

Mia (student) and F. Alejandra Cháker, CAS Coordinator, Colegio Gran Bretana, Bogotá, Colombia.

Creative experiences in CAS require students to produce either an original product or performance that is a result of creative thinking. There have been many fine examples from students who have sketched and produced their own exhibition of their work, written and performed their own songs and films or created flash mobs. Thinking creatively provides a clear link between thinking skills in the ATL and CAS.

ACTIVITY BOX
What creative thinking have you done for CAS?

9.02 Communication skills

Communication through interaction

CAS experiences provide many opportunities for students to interact with people with different life experiences and roles. In Salem College's Peterhof project, students learnt to interact with disabled people. This was quite demanding as the students did not speak Russian and many of the patients were quite severely disabled. This piece of reflection highlights the challenges faced:

CAS SNAPSHOT

'I started my morning by brushing the teeth of some adults in the Peterhof. We drew pictures with some disabled adults and I had to feed them at lunchtime again. The food did not seem to be very pleasant. I also went to the cafeteria to have some tea with some girls from my room. It was very nice! We also had some toast and cake.

Each student then took one disabled person and went outside with them. Most of them were in wheelchairs and we walked slowly to a small lake near the centre. The weather was very nice; the sun was shining and we fed the ducks with bread. The patients seemed to be very happy but unfortunately we had to go back after one hour as we had to bring the adults back to their rooms.'

Student at Salem College in Germany.

There are many other examples of students interacting with people outside their normal contacts and learning to communicate with them. Students at the Oak House School in Barcelona have worked with people from a totally different background who spoke mainly in Catalan; students from the New International School Thailand have worked with tribal villagers. These were face-to-face interactions. However, many student projects have involved students creating their own websites, as we saw with the 'Save the Perros' project in Chile (Chapter 2) and Jehona's project supporting the Mother Teresa Charity in Kosovo (see Chapter 8). In addition, students have created videos and posted them on YouTube. They can also interact with fellow students using Facebook pages or software such as Skype to plan and carry out CAS projects. These are practical ways of interacting with others for CAS.

SPOTLIGHT ON COMMUNICATION

Leading educators such as Tony Wagner, who has worked at Harvard University's Education programme and now consults around the world on the need for a change in the type of education needed for the twenty-first century, has identified the ability to communicate clearly as a key skill for the future (Wagner, 2014). This ability to communicate in both written and oral form using a number of different formats is something that has been identified as well by the US Government and by the ACTIS project (Binkley et al., 2010) as being essential. The following IB ATL specifies:

9

- The ability to communicate, in written or oral form, and understand, or make others understand, various messages in a variety of situations and for different purposes.

- The ability to listen to, and understand, various spoken messages in a variety of communicative situations, and to speak concisely and clearly.

- The ability to read and understand different texts, adopting strategies appropriate to various reading purposes (reading for information, for study or for pleasure) and to various text types.

- The ability to write different types of texts for various purposes. To monitor the writing process (from drafting to proofreading).

- The ability to formulate one's arguments, in speaking or writing, in a convincing manner and take full account of other viewpoints, whether expressed in written or oral form.

- The skills needed to use aids (such as notes, schemes, maps) to produce, present or understand complex texts in written or oral form (speeches, conversations, instructions, interviews, debates).

Each of these communication skills are used in CAS. You will have to articulate thoughts and ideas to CAS Advisors and Coordinators, service partners and fellow students to ensure that your planned experiences happen. Listening skills are important, no matter which of the three strands you are involved in, and being able to assess people that you are working with and their value sets is really important when working collaboratively with others.

In CAS you use the communication skills for all of the purposes mentioned above. We have also seen in Chapter 8 the importance of being able to use a variety of media to share and celebrate your achievements. One important aspect of CAS is that it can provide you with a chance to use your second or third language skills in carrying out CAS activities. This has mentioned as an important point by Oak House students in Barcelona.

ACTIVITY BOX

1 How are you using your second language for CAS?
2 How are you using ICT technology for CAS communications?

Using language to gather and communicate information

An important skill is being able to extract information in order to carry out a piece of research, either for a Service project or advocacy. Swiss students worked with the charity 'AIDS and Child'. On World AIDS day (1 December), the students raised awareness in their schools by researching about the causes and impacts of AIDS in Switzerland. They had the chance to meet Swiss victims of AIDS and discuss their experiences, such as how they felt and the impact of the medication they had to take. The interviews were often conducted in Swiss German, a dialect with which the students were not familiar. The students then prepared a presentation to use in other schools to discuss with fellow students the impact of AIDS on a personal level.

9.03 Social skills

The Collaborative for Academic, Social and Emotional Learning identifies five core social and emotional competencies which are all related to CAS:

Self-awareness: the ability to accurately recognise one's emotions and thoughts and their influence on behaviour. This includes accurately assessing one's strengths and limitations and possessing a well-grounded sense of confidence and optimism.

Self-management: the ability to regulate one's emotions, thoughts, and behaviours effectively in different situations. This includes managing stress, controlling impulses, motivating oneself, and setting and working toward achieving personal and academic goals.

Social awareness: the ability to take the perspective of, and empathise with, others from diverse backgrounds and cultures, to understand social and ethical norms for behaviour, and to recognise family, school, and community resources and supports.

Relationship skills: the ability to establish and maintain healthy and rewarding relationships with diverse individuals and groups. This includes communicating clearly, listening actively, cooperating, resisting inappropriate social pressure, negotiating conflict constructively, and seeking and offering help when needed.

Responsible decision making: the ability to make constructive and respectful choices about personal behaviour and social interactions based on consideration of ethical standards, safety concerns, social norms, the realistic evaluation of consequences of various actions, and the well-being of self and others.

Figure 9.3 Social and Emotional Skills for Life
(*www.casel.org/social-and-emotional-learning/core-competencies*)

Self-awareness and self-management

In the CAS Snapshot below, Manuel, a student from Colombia, describes how CAS helped him to combat a dislike and almost fear of playing sports. He had to participate in sport as part of a wider group activity on morals and ethics that was called 'Golombiao'. Manuel overcame his innate dislike of sports and came to realise the importance of commitment and involvement.

CAS SNAPSHOT

'Participating in these Golombiao sports activities was a whole new experience to me, as I have never really enjoyed group sports. I often feel like my teammates only integrate those players that are very skilled in the particular sport, and exclude those of us that aren't as skilled. Yet, playing soccer during Golombiao, I noticed that everyone was involved and interacted with each other, and being included into the game made me actually want to play better and participate more. After participating in these Golombiao activities I have come to realise that my initial antagonism towards group/team sports didn't arise wholly from the fact that the more skilled players excluded the rest, but also because I didn't participate enough or make sufficient effort for my teammates to see me as an integral member of the team. I am now more comfortable participating in team sports and I have even learnt to enjoy it, as I know that I don't have to be the most skilled player to be included in the team. I simply have to put effort into it and try my best, and others will be more willing to interact with me during the game.'

Manuela, Colegio Gran Bretaña, Bogotá, Colombia.

This is a good example of a student becoming aware of both physical and mental challenges they faced and working to overcome them. Manuel learned to manage his emotions and control them, something that many students face in a wide range of different activities. Often a student's body language will betray how they feel about carrying out a particular experience and this transmits itself to the people they are working with. These are moments when we need to exercise management of ourselves.

ACTIVITY BOX

1 Can you remember times when you have had to overcome challenges similar to Manuela's?
2 What steps have you taken to overcome fear?

Relationship skills and social awareness

Key point: In all three strands of CAS it is important that you are able to work effectively with others – this is also one of the learning outcomes for CAS. Another really important skill is developing a sense of empathy with people.

In Barcelona, the Oak House school works with a local group to help people in a poorer neighbourhood of the city. This project also demands social awareness.

CAS CASE STUDY

Bona Voluntat en Acció is a local non-profit organisation, which Oak House School has supported over the last few years. It is based in the Poble Sec district of Barcelona; this district has high levels of unemployment and residents have a mixed profile of elderly people and recent immigrants to Barcelona. *Bona Voluntat en Acció* collaborates with the local people in various ways, such as supporting 70 families from the district, supplying them with food donations each week, holding a weekly homework club for the children whose families are supported and finally, holding workshops and training sessions with the aim of equipping people with the vital skills to get into, or back into, the workplace.

Oak House students have been teaching adults basic English, focusing on conversation and language that can be used in the service industry. Oak House set up the classes two years ago and since then, students have volunteered to participate in the conversation classes on a weekly basis. The classes are held in the *Bona Voluntat en Acció* centre, which means that the Oak House students travel across town after school to assist with the classes.

Their responses in a group reflection highlights their ability to interact with others and establish some empathy.

a **What challenges did you expect to have, and how did you deal with them, and what challenges were unexpected, and how did you deal with them?**

'Interacting with students who are older than me is something I have never done before. Actually, I enjoyed the familiarity and closeness of the relationship. We were dealing with people who have never spoken another language, so one major challenge was pronunciation. There are sounds that are not at all similar, which I hadn't realised would be difficult. We dealt with this by encouraging repetition and writing things out in a phonetic way, finding similar sounds. We also used translation between the two languages.'

b   **What personal skills did you bring to the classes, and what do you feel were personal strengths that you could build on?**

'Being positive was important, because some of the students were people who, for one reason or another, find it hard not to give up. So it is important to encourage people. Also creating a good classroom atmosphere where people feel safe to learn was vital, as it helped the students to keep coming along to the classes. This became a place in which we could laugh together and enjoy each other's company.'

c   **You had to collaborate with a teacher that you knew, and adults that you did not know. In what way was the teaching a collaborative task?**

'The class was a sort of team situation, where our teachers Mrs McLatchie or Miss Harris led the different themes and we had to collaborate by teaching the same theme in small pairs. When Mrs McLatchie or Miss Harris taught new language points, they used us as models to practise questions and answers. So we needed to listen to our Oak House teacher, absorb and pass knowledge on. We had to pick up the signals in the class and collaborate.'

Students and the CAS Coordinator Mrs McLatchie from Oak House School, Barcelonaource.

This case study highlights many key aspects of working collaboratively with others, which is at the heart of CAS Service experiences. The students comment on the need to establish a relationship with the groups that they worked with in Barcelona, and how important it was to be positive with them. The quote of the students, 'We could laugh together and enjoy each other's company', clearly demonstrates both the empathy and the respect that they had for the people that they worked with. Moreover, the students also worked collaboratively with their teachers to deliver the lessons.

This book contains many examples of students working collaboratively with others for CAS. In the chapter on Celebration (Chapter 8) we had several examples of this, for example:

9

1 The 'Save the Perros' project in Chile students worked with a club to help establish awareness of stray dogs. Moreover, it was essential that the students worked with each other in building a website.

2 Jehona worked with colleagues in Zug to make bracelets to raise money for the Mother Teresa Charity in Kosovo.

3 The girls at Cheltenham Ladies' College worked with teachers and students to make up their wall of postcards for the 'Our Stories' project. This was a project that helped unify the school.

4 Thomas Vernacote spearheaded the imaginative 'Poems Through the Glass Walls' project that also embraced the whole school community at Brussels International School.

5 Diana Hoffbauer from Augsburg also highlighted the need for cooperative work with supervisors of disabled people.

ACTIVITY BOX

1 What challenges have you faced in collaborating with others in making a CAS project?
2 How have you overcome these problems of collaboration?
3 What have you learnt about collaboration with others from these experiences?

Responsible decision-making

A big challenge for many CAS students is that they want to be involved in service activities which they are not really qualified to do or participate in, in a meaningful way. This reflects a global problem where we want to help with but cannot because we do not yet have the skills to do so. A decision that has to be made is how can we help so that we make a meaningful contribution. This situation arose when a student was watching a television documentary.

CAS SNAPSHOT

A BBC television documentary reported on the lack of access to medical services in the rural part of the student's country of origin, India. The student's research revealed the NGO behind the 'Magic Train', called 'Impact India' that launched the world's first hospital on a train in 1991. With the service rendered by 80 000 surgeons for free, it has treated more than 800 000 poor people in rural India with sight, movement, hearing and cleft palate problems.

Through the help of her mother, the student met Impact India's CEO and discussed the possibility of helping out on the train. However, being a minor precluded her participation. Instead, she was introduced to an idea that later became her CAS project: 'Baby Wrap'. This required making quilts for babies born among tribes whose birthing practice upholds the natural separation of the newborns' umbilical cords from their mothers' placenta. During the process, however, babies often end up lying on the cold floor without any warm coverings. This has been strongly linked to the high rate of infant mortality in rural areas. Just one blanket would make a difference, and thousands of lives could be saved.

The student wasted no time in investigating what it took to make blankets for babies. Each blanket is made of 16 seven-inch cloth squares sewn together. Each square can be decorated with heartfelt messages and drawings. The decorated pieces are then sewn together by women who need to earn a living, supported by the Impact foundation. What materialised from this project were fun cloth-decorating sessions at lunch time at school that turned into quilts infused with warm, caring thoughts. The project had an impact on those who participated, and it is becoming a part of the school's annual events.

Here is a link to the YouTube advert made by the student and her collaborator: www.youtube.com/watch?v=jO72RaCSKRM&t=65.

Figure 9.4 An example of the quilts made for babies in India. *International School of Kuala Lumpur.*

Key point: Making responsible decisions in CAS comes down to being aware of what we are able to manage as students, and most importantly of the context that we work in. It does not matter which of the strands of CAS that we look at, we must be aware of the impact of our decisions on other people and the environment that we all share. This is both an ethical and practical issue. It links very strongly to a CAS learning outcome: Identify your own strengths and develop your weaknesses.

CAS Guide (2015) page 9

ACTIVITY BOX

Have you been in a situation where you have misjudged the context and made decisions based on this misjudgement?

9.04 Self-management skills

This skill category breaks down into two separate areas.

- Organisation skills — managing time and tasks effectively, goal-setting, etc.
- Affective skills — managing state of mind, self-motivation, resilience, mindfulness, etc.

IB ATL Skills (2015) IBO

Organisation

One of the things that causes anxiety to students is how they are going to fit CAS experiences into their life as well as studying. An interesting observation is that the academically most able students are often very good at time management. Some students that have obtained over 40 points in the IB Diploma Programme have managed to train and play sports three times a week, as well as participating in a play and helping a charity. They sit down and plan how their time will be used.

Complete the box below with your normal activities. Include the time spent for CAS, social and family life outside your normal school lessons. Make sure you allow at least one day off over the weekend. Monday has been filled in with examples.

Monday	Tuesday	Wednesday	Thursday	Friday	Saturday	Sunday
3.30–5.30 Sports training						
18–19.00 Dinner						
19–21.00						
21–23.00						

Goal setting is very important. At the start of your CAS programme – and when you are planning specific CAS experiences or projects – you need to be clear about what you want to achieve. That was evident in the planning of Thomas Verncote and his project of 'Poems Through the Glass Walls' (section 8.01); he was keen to emulate the poetry he had seen in London.

The three interviews that you are expected to have for CAS with your Coordinator should help you with goal setting. Remember to make your goals SMART:

S – Specific: very clearly worded and clear goals

M – Measurable: how can you tell whether you have achieved them or not?

A – Achievable: they are within your capabilities and time frame

R – Realistic: you are going to have the ability to realise them

T – Timely: the goals are going to be achieved within a clear time frame.

ACTIVITY BOX

State a SMART goal that you currently have for CAS.

9

Resilience

You will probably experience occasional setbacks if you have really challenged yourself in a CAS activity. A good example described earlier in this chapter is the group of students from Chile who tried to produce their own website. Twice the website crashed and they lost data. However, they did not give up; they managed to learn from their mistakes and were resilient, recovering from their setbacks and eventually finding a solution to their problems. It was the challenge of overcoming a temporary failure that made the task valuable for them. Resilience is a key part of being a risk-taker, because there will be times when things do not always work out as we think.

ACTIVITY BOX

Have you had situations where you have given up, or have chosen not to give up?

Self-motivation

This is key to success in CAS as in any other activity. Your own motivation to achieve something is always more effective in achieving your goals than any form of extrinsic motivation. One student said that he was determined to get fit enough to run a 42 km marathon as a CAS challenge. His father had promised him money if he could finish the marathon. However the student told his father that he wanted his father to donate the money to charity as it was not an incentive for him. The student duly managed to finish the marathon; at times he thought that this was not going to be possible, but he managed it. He discussed some of the challenges he faced after the run and said the challenge was mental as well as physical. The factor that helped him through this challenge was his motivation and desire to succeed.

ACTIVITY BOX

1   Without self-motivation we do not achieve anything that is really worthwhile. Do you agree with this statement?
2   How have you motivated yourself?

9.05 Research skills

Key point: Using good research skills can help you to find a CAS experience appropriate to your needs and skills. In many Service experiences you will need to carry out research to find out the real needs of a particular group and what you can do to help. This is also very important if you wish to carry out some advocacy for a particular cause or group.

Stu's Views

Figure 9.5 A cartoon about the importance of research skills and organisation.

9

Formulation and analysis of needs

In a Service activity, the needs of a group that you are collaborating with may change over time, and it is important that your efforts stay relevant to the project or experience. This has sometimes been a problem where a school has been working on a project for a long time overseas and has no way of reliably checking the needs of the local people.

When you are looking to work on a particular Service project, it is important to be clear on what help is needed, and this information comes from researching needs. Many times I have seen a huge drive to collect clothes for a particular group in need, and so much is collected that is not useful or relevant and then is simply sold on a local market.

Several of the service projects mentioned in this book have clearly carried out the research of the groups that they are working with. A good example is the student from the International School of Kuala Lumpur (section 9.03) who saw that the best way she could help babies in India was to make quilts for them. She was able to meet an authentic need.

ACTIVITY BOX

1   What research have you done before starting a CAS Service experience?
2   What different search engines have you used to help you?
3   Which is the most effective search engine for carrying out research for CAS?
4   How has research helped you to advocate for a particular cause or charity?

Location and evaluation of resources

When there is a natural disaster such as the Pacific tsunami in December 2004, the 2010 earthquake in Haiti or the tropical cyclone (hurricane) that swept through Vanuatu in 2015, many students want to help the victims. They will engage in huge fund-raising efforts but are often not sure of what to do with the money or goods they have collected. Following the devastating destruction of the 2004 tsunami, CAS students at one school (like many others globally) immediately launched a fund-raising campaign with a host of different activities including bake sales and creating special bracelets. In two weeks they raised over

$20 000, and then came the conundrum of what to do with the money. The students carried out some research on a number of charities and what they were doing to help in Aceh province and elsewhere. They quickly came to realise that some of the larger agencies were not being either effective or accountable for the funds that they had. Eventually they found a small charity that was working on the ground in Aceh and could show what they had done. Thus the students had learned to evaluate the various possibilities they had.

ACTIVITY BOX

Have you had to make a decision about what organisation or charity to support after a fund-raising campaign?

Key point: Making decisions about fund-raising is something that you should record in your CAS portfolio.

Recording and storage of information

An important requirement for your CAS portfolio (which has been discussed in Chapter 7) is how you are going to organise and store your CAS records and achievements. This is something that is important to think through before you start CAS.

Presentation and communication of CAS achievements

It is important to experiment a little and find different ways of communicating and celebrating your CAS achievements. There may be software for presenting information that you have not thought of; just try it and be a risk-taker.

ACTIVITY BOX

1 Have you thought of using padlet or other online software as a way of having a group reflection on an achievement? (Padlet is software freely available at www.padlet.com. It could be used to record reflections.)

2 What medium will you use to celebrate your achievements in CAS?

9.06 Review of Chapter 9

1. How do CAS and the ATL provide life skills?

2. When have communication skills been helpful with CAS experiences?

3. Why are thinking skills important for being successful?

4. In what ways do social skills developed in CAS help you with the academic courses in the Diploma Programme?

5. How has CAS helped you to develop your personal management skills?

6. Why are research skills important to CAS?

9.07 A summary of this chapter

- There are five major skills that have been identified as approaches to learning. They are communication, social, thinking, self-management and research.
- Each of these skills plays an important role in CAS.
- Critical and creative thinking skills are a vital part of CAS.
- Social skills are important for working with people in all three strands of CAS.
- Communications skills are essential to collaboration with others for service and carrying out a CAS project with others.
- Self-management is something that you have to learn in order to cope with the many demands of the Diploma Programme, and also to develop a good CAS programme.
- Research is part of the CAS stages model and a key part of CAS.

CAS and the
IB learner profile

10

The purpose of this chapter is to explain the close relationship between CAS and the IB learner profile. Understanding this relationship will help link your CAS experiences to the IB learner profile, apply the CAS aims to your work and clearly demonstrate in your portfolio that you have achieved the CAS learning outcomes.

Learner profile: according to the IB website, the 'IB learner profile is the IB mission statement translated into a set of learning outcomes for the 21st century'.

The first part of the chapter will give you an overview of the IB learner profile (10.01) and how it underpins the CAS aims (10.02). In addition, we will consider the close relationships between the learner profile and the CAS learning outcomes (10.03). Another important aspect of this chapter explores ways of analysing your CAS experiences in the light of the IB learner profile attributes (10.04), and lastly we shall look at the links between CAS, ethical education and the IB learner profile (10.05).

10.01 IB learner profile overview

The IB learner profile should be at the heart of your IB school environment: it should be referred to in posters on the classroom walls, on the school website, presentations at parents evenings, and so on. Every teacher will be talking about it, but it is worth asking a key question:

ACTIVITY BOX

What does the IB learner profile mean to you?

The IB learner profile ten attributes are:

- Inquirers
- Knowledgeable
- Thinkers

- Communicators
- Principled
- Open-minded

- Caring
- Risk-takers
- Balanced
- Reflective.

International Baccalaureate Organization (2013)

These attributes represent the core values of an IB community, and are the skills, attitudes and values that will help you become a well-rounded, balanced person.

They address the following areas in your education:

- Intellectual (knowledgeable, thinkers, reflective)
- Emotional (caring, risk-takers, balanced)
- Social/cultural (communicators, open-minded)
- Ethical and spiritual (inquirers, principled).

Figure 10.1 Creating the perfect balance: the image represents the balance achieved with contributions from different parts of the IB core values, each one playing a unique role.

ACTIVITY BOX

If you could add another attribute, what would it be – and why?

10

10.02 CAS aims and the IB learner profile

The CAS programme aims to develop you into someone who is able to:

- Enjoy and find significance in a range of CAS experiences
- Purposefully reflect upon their experiences
- Identify goals, develop strategies and determine further actions for personal growth
- Explore new possibilities, embrace new challenges and adapt to new roles
- Actively participate in planned, sustained and collaborative CAS projects
- Understand they are members of local and global communities with responsibilities towards each other and the environment.

CAS Guide (2015), page 10

ACTIVITY BOX

Figure 10.2 provides some suggested links between the CAS aims and the IB learner profile attributes.

Copy and complete the chart to include all ten learner attributes – you may agree or disagree with the given example. Which of the learning outcomes do you think would be easy for you to achieve? Which would take you out of your comfort zone? You can write your ideas at the end of each arrow.

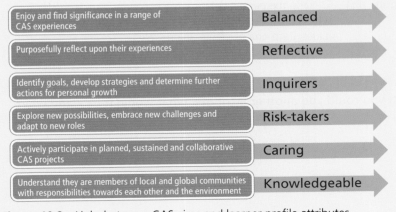

Figure 10.2 Links between CAS aims and learner profile attributes.

10.03 CAS learning outcomes and the IB learner profile

The CAS learning outcomes are derived from the IB learner profile and form the backbone of the CAS programme. To successfully complete your CAS programme, you must provide evidence in your CAS portfolio that you have achieved all seven CAS learning outcomes. Much of that evidence will come from reflection on your CAS experiences and projects.

> **Key point:** 'Some learning outcomes may be achieved many times, while others may be achieved less frequently'.
> *CAS Guide* (2015), page 11

Let's take a look at these word cloud images. Figure 10.3 incorporates all the CAS learning outcomes, and Figure 10.4 contains the learner profile attributes.

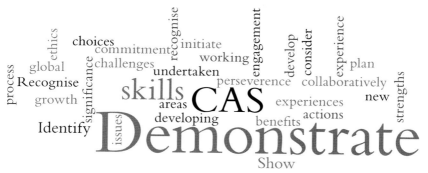

Figure 10.3 A word cloud of CAS learning outcomes.

Figure 10.4 A word cloud of IB learner profile attributes.

10

Complete the second column of Table 10.1, matching the relevant learner profile attribute(s) to the CAS learning outcomes.

CAS learning outcomes	IB learner profile attributes
Identify your own strengths and develop areas for growth	
Demonstrate that challenges have been undertaken, developing new skills in the process	
Demonstrate how to initiate and plan a CAS experience	
Show commitment to and perseverance in CAS experiences	
Demonstrate the skills and recognise the benefits of working collaboratively	
Demonstrate engagement with issues of global significance	
Recognise and consider the ethics of choices and actions	

Table 10.1   CAS learning outcomes and IB learner profiles.

10.04 CAS experiences and the IB learner profile

Key point: 'A CAS experience must provide opportunities to develop the attributes of the IB learner profile.'

CAS Guide (2015), page 15

CAS CASE STUDY

In this student reflection example, we have highlighted in yellow the IB learner profile attributes that have been developed, without having been explicitly named by the student. The numbers refer to the attributes listed on page 244.

InterCAS – reflection

'During my short life, I have lived through many fulfilling experiences. Yet, none of them has been quite so rewarding as my work a few months ago in the Inter-CAS Ambato 2014. I went without knowing the benefits that it would give me to change my future (1) and particularly to every child who has autism; like my other classmates we immersed ourselves in this worldwide topic (2), which was full of obstacles but also beautiful memories that we will cherish in our hearts.

'After spending fascinating days learning about the Autistic Spectrum Disorder (ASD) (3) and the help that the therapy dogs provide both to children and young people, I was able to observe the reality that the majority of people with autism are living within our society (4). This society is very closed and does not accept people who are classified as disabled just because they are different from those who classify themselves as "normal", without realising that everyone in this world is different and that a condition of life, such as autism, should not exclude them from being treated with equality, respect and love (5).

'The work we did in Ambato was of immense benefit. We had the chance to get to know a small part of my country, what ASD is and the qualities of the children that are born with this condition. I am already excited to know that there are now many more people who are aware of this issue of global importance (6), with adolescents, parents and adults getting involved in the struggle for people with ASD so that they may have all the rights they deserve and can be integrated into our society (7). Although they are listed as a vulnerable group, their strength and tenacity go way beyond what most "normal" people have.

'During the time we spent together, the autistic people I met gave me a huge lesson in life (8); they do not want to be cured from autism because it is not a disease. They want us to look at what is going on around us, stop being so selfish and help those who are suffering in silence and experiencing crises when they can no longer shoulder their burden (9); the gaze that we give them is not to exclude but to make them part of each one of us. Even though many of them do not speak, they do have feelings and, with their eyes, they express all their emotions, fears (10) and the circumstances that are making them uncomfortable. Therefore, now that I look at them I realise that love is unconditional and the children with autism are willing to offer me this type of caring (11). It is an unconventional affection due to the lack of communication, but it is enduring and just as strong as any other displays of affection, transcending all barriers.

10

'Inter-CAS removed the bandages from my eyes (12) and now I can proudly say that I have changed to appreciating that a condition of life does not make us lesser human beings. On the contrary, we must work with great effort and passion for those who are excluded because they are vulnerable (13). For this reason, I am grateful to the people who made possible this event that has helped the children with ASD; I am convinced that this was the first great step to their inclusion in our society, and that everyone will see how great it is to have a link to these children.'

Donatella, Colegio Politécnico, Guayaquil, Ecuador.

The attributes shown in this example:

1 Risk-takers
2 Inquirers
3 Knowledgeable
4 Caring
5 Reflective
6 Knowledgeable
7 Principled

8 Communicators
9 Balanced
10 Communicators
11 Thinkers
12 Open-minded
13 Principled.

This is a good example of how much you can derive from your CAS experience. It also shows how to identify your achievements, and highlight your skills and accomplishments in your portfolio.

We strongly suggest that you do the same exercise with your own reflections in Table 10.2. Not only will it help to develop awareness of your reflection skills, it will keep a tight focus on what you are doing and why. This is an example of being able to see the links between your experience and the values of the IB stated in two different areas (this is called metacognition, and developing this skill is an important ATL).

Your CAS experience	Connect the two	IB learner profile attributes

Table 10.2   Connecting your CAS experiences with learner profile attributes.

10

10.05 CAS, the IB learner profile and ethical education

The relationship between values and behaviour is complex. For our own values to really come to life, they should carry through to all the things that we do. If we do not live our values, they become just nice words with no real implication for the choices we make.

The IB learner profile is the set of values that represent the ethics of the International Baccalaureate Organization. As members of the IB community, we are all encouraged to develop the IB learner profile attributes as our common ground.

A brief introduction to ethical education

Ethical education: the process of building a solid ethical identity, in other words developing a moral conscience that guides our actions.

Ethical education aims to encourage:

- The development of an ethical identity that is free, independent, responsible and able to take ethically valid decisions
- A respectful and peaceful coexistence among people, groups, cultures and countries
- Intercultural understanding that safeguards the identity of people and communities and celebrates diversity.

It is the beginning of a life-long journey of personal growth, which:

- Develops ethical capacities, involving thinking, feeling, perceiving, behaving, and seeking personal fulfilment and community welfare
- Fosters the capacity to understand and behave appropriately in real-life situations
- Is achieved through experiential learning.

It develops students' ethical intelligence, which is composed of abilities such as:

- Self-awareness and self-esteem
- Empathy
- Communication
- Consideration of the ethical implications before action
- Sensitivity
- Critical understanding
- Cooperation
- Decision-making and problem-solving skills
- Self-regulation.

One of the CAS learning outcomes, 'recognize and consider the ethics of choices and actions', specifically encourages you to address the ethical issues, such as those listed above, which will arise during your CAS experiences. When doing this you should be guided by the ethical principles contained in the IB Mission Statement and the IB learner profile.

Your CAS experiences will provide many opportunities for you to shape your ethical identity – in other words to develop your own value system, to explore your own attitudes and behaviours, to analyse your opinions and actions, and to find your own place in the world.

When choosing the experiences and projects for your CAS programme, bear in mind that they should develop your abilities and skills in the following areas:

- Independence of thought and action
- Reflection
- Dialogue
- Open-mindedness
- Commitment
- Responsible participation
- Accountability
- Social responsibility
- Social development
- Respect for human rights
- International mindedness.

10

Reflect on your CAS experiences and fill in Table 10.3.

Skill	CAS experience that demonstrates this
Independent thought and action (what actions and ideas have you had about CAS as an individual)	
Dialogue (your ability to communicate and discuss with others)	
Open-mindedness	
Commitment/responsible participation	
Accountability	
Social responsibility (awareness of community needs)	
Social development (ability to get on with others)	
Respect for others' human rights	
International mindedness	

Table 10.3   Skills demonstrated during CAS experiences.

CAS CASE STUDY

Here is a final reflection from a school in Bogotá, Colombia, which sums up how CAS can transform the whole school community life. The reflection shows that at the core of any school is the way that we act and behave towards each other in the school, local and global community. In particular, we can learn so much from practical service where we get our hands dirty by doing something with others to improve life. CAS provides that opportunity and helps to give true meaning to the IB Mission statement. It is for this reason that CAS should be at the core of any IB school.

Colegio Gran Bretaña's CORE

An approach to the experience of CAS within an internationally minded community

'The word CORE defines the essential nature and individuality of *something*. This *something* could be us. However, our identity is not defined by social constructs such as our profession, name or nationality, but by our actions. Our actions arise from that impulse that makes us act in a given situation. To know how to act, we must feed and nurture our minds, hearts and bodies constantly throughout our life. That *something* that we feed is our centre, our core.

'CAS is becoming the core of the Colegio Gran Bretaña in Bogotá, Colombia since it is constantly evolving, enriched by the experience and knowledge of the teachers and by the skills developed in our students throughout the school year. See section 9.01 for more details of their project Screencast, combining English, Art and Technology.

'We also encourage our students to become service-minded through service projects such as *La Manuelita* (held outside the school at an elder's house) and the *Health Brigade* (an annual event that provides medical check-ups to CAZUCA, a community supported by CGB). Both projects involve our entire community and promote collaborative work, and give students the opportunity to actively experience global citizenship.

'CGB also looks for innovation, inquiry and curiosity in their pupils. To do this we have begun the *Golombiao* project through an alliance with the organisation *Colombia Joven* and UNICEF here in Bogotá (see section 9.03 for a student's personal experience of *Golombiao*).

'This project teaches students about their rights and responsibilities, giving them the tools to promote respect, reach out to the wider community, relate to others, break down social barriers and understand what it is to be part of one world – one community.

'This is how CAS could be described at Colegio Gran Bretaña in Bogotá, Colombia: life-changing, service-minded and learning through authentic life experiences.'

This reflection shows IB students working together in a CAS experience. It is a symbol of what CAS is all about: learning by action and reflecting on that action; experiential learning that contributes to the development of ethical identity; the IB Mission statement and the IB leaner profile put into practice.

Figure 10.5 Working together for CAS.

10

10.06 Review of Chapter 10

1 What for you are the most important points raised in this chapter?

2 Which of the IB learner profile attributes do you think would be most difficult to develop? Why?

3 How can a CAS experience help to develop the IB learner profile attributes?

4 In what ways can you develop your ethical identity through your CAS experiences?

10.07 A summary of this chapter

In this chapter we have:

- Addressed an overview of the IB learner profile
- Explored how the IB learner profile has inspired the CAS aims
- Considered the strong relationships between the learner profile attributes and CAS learning outcomes
- Explored ways of analysing your CAS experiences in the light of the IB learner profile attributes
- Looked at some of the links between CAS, ethical education and the IB learner profile.

Glossary

Action plan: an outline of tasks that need to be completed in order to achieve a defined goal, who will complete them, and when they are to be completed by.

Activity: 'physical exertion contributing to a healthy lifestyle'.

CAS Guide (2015)

Areas of knowledge (AOK): these are specific branches of knowledge, each of which has a distinct nature and uses different methods of gaining knowledge. TOK distinguishes between eight areas of knowledge: mathematics, the natural sciences, the human sciences, the arts, history, ethics, religious knowledge systems, and indigenous knowledge systems.

TOK Guide (2013)

CAS experience: an event that you will count as part of your CAS. It may be a series of events, such as training and being in a team, or practising and then taking part in a performance, or it may be a one-off event such as marshalling a sports event, or a weekend mountain-biking.

CAS personal profile: this is a summary of your interests, skills, talents and areas that you would like to develop. It can help you to think about your CAS programme as a coherent activity that fits together, perhaps with your career or university goals.

CAS portfolio: a collection of your CAS planning, reflections, and evidence of CAS involvement and achievements.

CAS programme: a number of combined experiences that you undertake throughout your time studying the IB Diploma Programme. Some are large, in-depth experiences combining many events, while others are smaller, one-off events. Some programmes have many experiences, some have few.

CAS project: a 'collaborative, well-considered series of sequential CAS experiences, engaging students in one or more of the CAS strands of creativity, activity, and service'.

CAS Guide (2015)

CAS stages: a framework to assist students in planning and carrying out their CAS experiences / projects. The five stages are Investigation, Preparation, Action, Reflection and Demonstration.

Creativity: 'exploring and extending ideas leading to an original or interpretive product or performance'.

CAS Guide (2015)

Development of an ethical identity: becoming the author of your own life. It includes evaluating and decision-making skills.

Ethical education: the process of building a solid ethical identity, in other words developing a moral conscience that guides our actions.

Ethics: also referred to as moral philosophy, 'involves systematising, defending, and recommending concepts of right and wrong behaviour'.

Fieser, n.d.

Experiential education: a philosophy of education where students become actively involved in the learning process. It is learning by action and reflecting on that action.

Experiential learning: learning from experience; enhancing the understanding gained from an experience through reflection.

Global issue: issues of public significance or concern that manifest in local and worldwide contexts

InterCAS: conferences held in various countries, especially in South America, which bring together students and CAS Coordinators from a large number of schools to learn about a particular theme for CAS and to share CAS experiences and achievements together.

International mindedness: the knowledge and understanding of self and other cultures that allows for positive interaction; what some may refer to as global citizenship or global competencies.

Knowledge question: a carefully devised question that leads to inquiry about claims about knowledge, and about knowledge itself. It is a core learning tool in TOK.

Learner profile: according to the IB website, the 'IB learner profile is the IB mission statement translated into a set of learning outcomes for the 21st century'.

Linear process: a process that progresses straight from one stage to another, with a starting point and an ending point.

Needs analysis: a technique used to gather information about the needs of a community or group, focusing on the issues or problems faced in that group. The needs refer to gaps or areas of concern; things that are needed to help better support that community.

NGO: Non-government organisation, also referred to as non-profit, is a community group which is not a part of government or for-profit business sectors. NGOs may provide you with a community partner for CAS service activities.

Press release: also referred to as a media release, this is a written statement or article provided to media outlets announcing certain details of a newsworthy event.

Project-based learning: focused on real-life situations and challenges, and relies on investigation, decision-making and problem-solving skills.

Reciprocity: in the context of service in CAS, the process where both parties in a service setting gain positively from the experience.

Reflection: 'Experience is not what happens to you; it's what you do with what happens to you'.

Aldous Huxley

Relationship skills: the ability to establish and maintain healthy and rewarding relationships with diverse individuals and groups. This includes communicating clearly, listening actively, cooperating, resisting inappropriate social pressure, negotiating conflict constructively, and seeking and offering help when needed.

www.casel.org

Responsible decision-making: the ability to make constructive and respectful choices about personal behaviour and social interactions based on consideration of ethical standards, safety concerns, social norms, the realistic evaluation of consequences of various actions, and the well-being of self and others.

www.casel.org

Self-awareness: the ability to accurately recognise one's emotions and thoughts and their influence on behaviour. This includes accurately assessing one's strengths and limitations and possessing a well-grounded sense of confidence and optimism.

www.casel.org

Self-management: the ability to regulate one's emotions, thoughts, and behaviours effectively in different situations. This includes managing stress, controlling impulses, motivating oneself, and setting and working toward achieving personal and academic goals.

www.casel.org

Service: the act of doing something for the benefit of others or for the greater good. Defined in the *CAS Guide* (2015) as 'Collaborative and reciprocal engagement with the community in response to an authentic need'.

Service learning: is 'a philosophy, pedagogy, and model for community development that is used as an instructional strategy to meet learning goals and/or content standards'.

National Youth Leadership Council, 2008

SMART goals: A set of criteria to follow so that you can help make your goals a reality. Goals should be Specific, Measurable, Attainable, Realistic and Timely.

Social awareness: the ability to take the perspective of and empathise with others from diverse backgrounds and cultures, to understand social and ethical norms for behavior, and to recognise family, school, and community resources and supports.

www.casel.org

Strands: refers to the three areas of CAS that gives this programme its name: Creativity, Activity, Service. All CAS experiences must fall within one of the three strands.

TED: is an abbreviation of Technology, Education and Design. A TEDx event is a local gathering where live TED-like talks and videos previously recorded at TED conferences are shared with the community. TEDx events are fully planned and coordinated independently, on a community-by-community basis. The content and design of each TEDx event is unique and developed independently, but all of them have features in common (www.ted.com/participate/organize-a-local-tedx-event/before-you-start/what-is-a-tedx-event).

WOK: the TOK course identifies eight specific ways of knowing (WOKs). They are: language, sense perception, emotion, reason, imagination, faith, intuition and memory.

TOK Guide (2013)

References

Publications

Approaches to Teaching and Learning in the Diploma Programme (2015) IBO

Cannings J., Innes Piaggio M. and Money S. (2013), *CAS Illustrated*. IBO: Geneva.

CASEL (2013), *Social and Emotional Core Competencies*, available at www.casel.org/social-and-emotional-learning/core-competencies

Furco, A. (1996), '"Service Learning": A Balanced Approach to Experiential Education', *Expanding Boundaries: Service and Learning*. Washington DC: Corporation for National Service, 26.

Gibbs, G. (1988), *Learning by Doing*. Oxford: Oxford Polytechnic.

International Baccalaureate (2012), *TOK Guide*. Cardiff: International Baccalaureate.

International Baccalaureate (2013), *Extended Essay Guide*. Cardiff: International Baccalaureate.

International Baccalaureate (2015), *CAS Teacher Support Material*. The Hague: International Baccalaureate.

International Baccalaureate (May 2015, May 2012, May 2009, May 2007), *TOK Essay Titles*. Cardiff: International Baccalaureate.

International Baccalaureate Organization (2015). *CAS Teacher Support Material*. Geneva: IBO.

International Baccalaureate Organisation (2015), *Creativity, Action, Service Guide*. IBO: Geneva.International Baccalaureate Organisation (2013), *Theory of Knowledge Guide*. IBO: Geneva.

Kolb, D.A. (1984), *Experiential Learning: Experience as the Source of Learning and Development*. Englewood Cliffs, NJ: Prentice Hall.

National Youth Leadership Council (NYLC) (2008), *K-12 Service-Learning Standards for Quality Practice, 2008*.

Peterson, A. (2003), *Schools Across Frontiers: The Story of the International Baccalaureate and the United World Colleges.* Chicago, IL: Open Court Publishing Company.

Rischard, J.F. (2002), *High Noon: 20 Global Problems, 20 Years to Solve Them.* New York: Basic Books.

Rogers, C. and H. Jerome Frieberg (1994). *Freedom to Learn.* Englewood Cliffs, NJ: Prentice Hall (3rd edition).

Rutherford, J. et al. (2014), *IB Theory of Knowledge Skills and Practice.* Oxford: Oxford University Press.

Singh, M. and Qi, J. (2013), *21st Century International Mindedness: An Exploratory Study of its Conceptualisation and Assessment.* Research Paper for the IB, University of West Sydney, pages 13–14.

The Development Education Association (2010), *Unlocking the Educational Potential of Fundraising Activities: Guidelines for Good Practice in Fundraising with Young People.*

Binkley, M., Erstad, O., Herman, J., Raizen, S., Ripley, M. and Rumble, M. (2010) *Defining 21st Century skills,* available at http://cms.education.gov.il/NR/rdonlyres/19B97225-84B1-4259-B423-4698E1E8171A/115804/defining21stcenturyskills.pdf

Wagner, T. (2014) *Play, passion, purpose: Tony Wagner at TEDxNYED,* available at www.youtube.com/watch?v=hvDjh4l-VHo

Website resources

Fieser, J. (n.d.). *Ethics.* Retrieved from: http://www.iep.utm.edu/ethics/.

http://helpingthemotherteresasociety.weebly.com/

www.ibo.org/en/programmes/diploma-programme/curriculum/extended-essay/world (Accessed 1 March 2015)